KYUDO

弓道

KYUDO
THE WAY OF THE BOW

FELIKS HOFF

TRANSLATED BY
Sherab Chödzin Kohn

SHAMBHALA
Boston & London 2002

Shambhala Publications, Inc.
Horticultural Hall
300 Massachusetts Avenue
Boston, Massachusetts 02115
www.shambhala.com

Previously published as *Kyudo: Die Kunst des japanischen
Bogenschießens* ©1999 by Verlag Weinmann—Berlin
English translation ©2002 by Shambhala Publications, Inc.
Title page calligraphy by Kaji Aso

9 8 7 6 5 4 3 2 1

First Edition

Printed in the United States of America

♾ This edition is printed on acid-free paper that meets
the American National Standards Institute Z39.48 Standard.

Distributed in the United States by Random House, Inc.,
and in Canada by Random House of Canada Ltd

Library of Congress Cataloging-in-Publication Data
Hoff, Feliks.
[Kyudo. English]
Kyudo : the way of the bow / Feliks Hoff ; translated by Sherab Chödzin
Kohn.—1st ed.
p. cm.
Includes bibliographical references
ISBN 1-57062-852-1
1. Archery—Japan. I.Title.
GV1188.J3 H642002
799.3'2'0952—dc21   2001055524

CONTENTS

PREFACE

WHEN, IN THE AUTUMN of 1969, I had my
first encounter with Inagaki Sensei and kyudo, I was by no means
conscious of my possible role as the author of a book on kyudo.
Only when I was urged by interested people from Hamburg, and
later by people from other cities in Germany, to provide an introduction to, and instruction in, the Way of the Bow, did it become
clear to me that a learning manual was needed as an aid for individuals and small groups practicing this art in relative isolation.

The original document was a description of the basic technique. This served the German kyudo community for nine years
as a theoretical foundation for its exercises; it was constantly
added to over the years.

Anyone working in one of the budo arts knows from experience that a state of mind very frequently arises in which we believe
that we have at last understood just about all there is to understand about the discipline. But if we continue diligently with the
practice, we soon discover new dimensions beyond what we have
already learned—for the most part more challenging ones that
initially we were not capable even of perceiving or of compre-
hending at all, much less of executing or relating to in a living way.

In putting together a German kyudo book, over time a multitude of questions and problems came up concerning content,
level of detail, method of presenting text and graphics, and so on.
No book usable as a practice manual existed yet in a European

language. For this reason, recourse to the Japanese material— naturally the best and most authentic source—seemed advisable. In presenting this book today to the kyudo community, I must acknowledge that in the last analysis I have only passed on what I myself was able to learn through love and patience from my teacher, Genshiro Inagaki, eighth dan hanshi. The book is far from containing everything there is to be said on the subject, but kyudo is above all a path of concrete experience gathered on one's own, and so this text can be no more than a support and aid for those who have committed themselves to this path.

The chapters offered here were composed with the intention of providing a working basis for practical kyudo training as well as a brief presentation of information about kyudo equipment and ideas. I would like especially to draw attention to chapters 10, "Basic Technique of the Heki School," and 13, "Correcting Common Mistakes." Reading this material in tandem with actual practice will help the archer to gain significant insights into his or her technique.

I should not neglect at this point to thank all those who, through their encouragement and help, have supported my work on this book. My thanks go first of all to Inagaki Sensei, who was kind enough to permit chapter 5 from his book *Kyudo Nyomon* to be translated here (see chapter 13, "Correcting Common Mistakes"). In addition, Inagaki Sensei composed the essay "Yumi no kokoro" especially for this book, and also allowed us to use here parts of a transcription of a talk of his on the history of kyudo.

I would like to thank Dr. Manfred Speidel, who reviewed the manuscript and translated and revised the talks by Inagaki Sensei for the original German edition. Further thanks go to the Studio Flossel and kyudo practitioners Arend Brandt, Cornelia Brandl, Jürgen Fritsch, and Angela Neumeister for their kind collaboration in the preparation of the photos and the manuscript as well as the glossary. I also thank Dr Weinmann for his participation as publisher of the original German edition.

I would like to express my personal expectations for this book by means of a Japanese poem, which can be translated more or less as follows:

My bow and I are drawn to the full,
How far will the arrow fly?
I do not know.

KYUDO

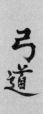

1

A BRIEF HISTORY OF KYUDO

THE ART AND CULT of archery are nearly as old as humanity itself. As a weapon, the bow surpassed in range and effectiveness the sling, the spear, and the blowgun—and, like the gods themselves, it brought death from afar, without the archer having to make himself visible to his target. In addition, the bow served from the earliest days of humanity not only as a weapon for hunting and war, but also as an apparatus for kindling fire. Finally, its plucked string was the origin from which certain string musical instruments developed.

The most ancient arrowheads are estimated to be over fifty thousand years old. Cave drawings dating from ten thousand years ago depict hunters of the Middle Stone Age shooting bows. In more recent times, stories of archery and archers pervaded all cultural areas. Odysseus wreaked his revenge on the suitors with his bow. Xerxes threatened the Greeks by declaring that his arrows would darken the heavens—a remark that purportedly prompted enemy King Leonidas to reply: "Then we'll fight in the shade!" Among equestrian peoples of Asia, the main weapons were bows whose penetrating power was so great that a direct hit could pierce any shield or armor. But even dense flights of arrows, not fired directly at specific targets, as well as fire and poisoned arrows, had dire effects in many a battle. A clear depiction of the use of the bow and arrow for sending signals is found in a famous thirteenth-century Chinese novel, in which a robber called Beach Signal Arrow shoots arrows that make a sound.*

The bow and arrow survived the invention of the crossbow in the eleventh century and the first handguns around 1520, because a good archer could shoot a bow thirty-six times in the interval it took to load and fire a harquebus and could initially surpass the gunpowder-fired weapons in range and accuracy.

The longest shot ever recorded was by Sultan Selim III in 1798 in Constantinople. The distance covered was 972 yards and 2½ inches, or about 900 meters. The current record is around 700 meters, which proves that even modern materials cannot outperform the artfully constructed Turkish reflex bow made from bull-neck sinew and horn. One must also acknowledge the record of the Japanese archer Yamada Gumbe, who shot a distance of 450 meters with his kyudo bow, a record for a bow of this type.

In Europe, for the most part only the French and English used archery in war. However, it was the Poles who, in a battle against Napoleon in 1807, used the bow for the last time for military purposes.

Archers from throughout the world engaged in the first peaceful competition at the Paris Olympic Games of 1900, and the event was repeated in 1904, 1908, and 1920. Then, after a long hiatus, this classical weapon appeared once again in the competitions

* The author cites *Die Räuber vom Liang Schan Moor* (The Bandits of Liang Shan Marsh), translated from the Chinese by Franz Kuhn. The original Chinese work is ascribed to Shi Nai'an (ca. 1290–ca. 1365) and Luo Guanzhong (ca. 1330–ca. 1400). An English version is *Outlaws of the Marsh*, 2 vols., translated by Sidney Shapiro (Bloomington: Indiana University Press, 1981).

–Editor

for Olympic honors at the 1972 games in Munich. Western-style archery is of course now a regular part of the games.

The Japanese tradition of archery now known as kyudo (*kyu* = bow, *do* = way) includes within it just about everything that has ever arisen in the history of human interaction with the "feathered death." We find ceremonial forms, conjuring techniques, and techniques for constructing and shooting the bow. Finally, all this was shaped aesthetically and philosophically by the ideas of Shinto and Zen. Matches and competitive forms of kyudo that bear witness to this earlier history continue to exist right up to the present day.

We find the first representations of the kyudo bow, with its proportions of two above to one below the hand grip, in bronzes from the third century. Also, ancient Chinese history texts state that the people of the land of "Wa" (Japan) used bows of this sort. Written evidence from this period is sparse. During the Kofun period (300–645), the bow was used as a hunting weapon and was also offered to the gods as a sacred phallic symbol of strength. An account from this early time tells us that Mutoku Tenno from Korea possessed an iron shield that was pierced by a Japanese arrow.

In the Hakuho period (645–710), under the influence of Confucianist China, archery was introduced into the court, where it was used as an element in a variety of ceremonies. This period in Japan came just after the introduction of Buddhism into the country by Prince Shotoku Taishi (574–622), who is also considered the founder of the first school of Japanese archery, the Taishi Ryu (*ryu* = school).

But court philosophy was too complicated for the simple people who used the bow as a weapon for hunting and war (fig. 1.1). The political developments of the Heian period (794–1184) brought about the formation of small bands of warriors, or *bushi*, under whose influence archery and the other martial arts were greatly developed and refined. The following Kamakura period (1185–1395) brought increasing importance to the bushi, who later came to be known as samurai. Various political and social factors contributed to their finally becoming the ruling class. During the Kamakura period, the sword-wielding warrior was regarded as the paragon, but the abbreviation *kyu ba so ken* (bow, horse, spear, sword), which also derives from this period, provides an indication of what martial arts were being daily exercised by the bushi. The ideas of Zen Buddhism were introduced from China during this period, and the philosophy and code of the *bushido* (Way of the Knight) came into being. This development occurred despite the fact that the period up till the end of the sixteenth century was so filled with civil wars that the average samurai rarely had an opportunity to engage in anything more peaceful than fighting. Until well into the Tokugawa period (1600–1868), the concept of *jutsu* (technique, art) was dominant in the martial arts. During the long period of peace under the Tokugawa, out of *kenjutsu* (the art of the sword) there arose *kendo* (the Way of the Sword); and from the technical art of archery arose the Way of the Bow, an existential discipline shaped by Zen ideas. The notion of kyudo appeared significantly earlier than terms for the Ways arising from the other arts of the bushi. In 1660 Morikawa Kosan, a kyudo master who became the founder of the Yamato Ryu, used this concept for the first time.

FIGURE I.I.
Courtiers and Sugawara Michizane doing archery. Detail from a pictorial scroll, 1219.

The likely reason for the appearance of the concept of kyudo is that in 1542 the Portuguese in Tanegashima sold the local daimyo the first fuse-fired muskets, thus ushering in a new era of Japanese military technique. The use of a rifle could be quickly learned, whereas long training was needed for the sword and the bow. Moreover, firearms could be manufactured easily and far more cheaply than hand-forged swords. All in all, this made firearms the perfect weapon for the army of Oda Nobunaga, which was mainly recruited from the peasantry. With only three thousand muskets, this army was able to wipe out a traditional samurai cavalry in the battle of Nagashino. Apparently, Nobunaga's army in 1575 was more advanced in musketry maneuvers than any armed forces in Europe. From that time on, though bows continued to be used for sport, play, and ceremony, archery lost its importance as a military art.

Owing to the strict regimentation of social classes during the Tokugawa shogunate, the samurai found themselves obliged to study classical writings and to continue to practice the traditional martial arts, though there was no longer any direct need for them. In addition, the question of a sudden decision between life and death remained, independent of periods of war, an ongoing problem for the bushi. Because of their unique conception of loyalty and honor, individual fights were not avoided during this period. However, the problem of life and death, looked at from a technical point of view, was a problem of winning or losing. Often the most difficult opponent, the greatest problem that had to be overcome lest the warrior be defeated by it, was *the warrior himself.* The existentially important question this presented for the samurai could only be solved if he succeeded in creating a world that sought the absence of combat and communicated a sense of peace.

In the context of the martial arts, this means attaining a state of mastery so great that it can transcend life and death and react as needed with a higher technique. Anyone who, as a result of this achievement, no longer has to reckon with defeat becomes unopposed and loses his enemies. He has reached the state of no-combat.

In the fifteenth century a samurai appeared who was seen as a divine manifestation, the legendary Heki Danjo Masatsugu, the founder of the Heki Ryu, from which the Izumo, Sekka, Insai, Dosetsu, Chikurin, and Okura groups are derived.

A century earlier, Ogasawara Sadamune had introduced the ceremony of shooting the bow to the court of the Godaigo Tenno. The founder of the present Ogasawara Ryu was Sadamune's fifth-generation successor, Ogasawara Nagakyo.

Genshiro Inagaki is at present the master of the Insai group of the Heki school (Heki Ryu Insai Ha). If we trace his lineage back through his teacher Urakami Sakae and the latter's father, Urakami Naoki, we come, at the beginning of the seventeenth century, to the master of the Insai Ha school, Yoshida Genhachiro Shigeuji (thirteenth generation after Heki Danjo). In Yoshida's writings, Heki Danjo Masatsugu is presented as the incarnation of Hachiman Daibosatsu, the "great bodhisattva Hachiman," the war god (fig. 1.2).

FIGURE 1.2. *The war god Hachiman with bow and arrows. Wooden figure in the temple gate of the Toshugu Shrine in Nikko.*

History recounts that he was born in Yamato, distinguished himself in the battle of Uchino (Iga), wandered through the provinces in order to teach his art to the peasants, who could not afford a horse for battle, and finally became a priest on Mount Koya at the age of fifty-nine.

In the battle of Uchino, history tells us, Heki Danjo routed his enemies with his war cry alone and won the fight without a single fatality. Heki was famous for the fact that every arrow that he shot with the battle cry *"Eiiii!"* was certain to pierce one or even two enemy soldiers, and when he aimed at the enemy soldiers, they already saw themselves pierced by Heki's arrows and became immobile, so that they were no longer able to shoot arrows themselves. At Uchino, Heki's voice alone was enough. Not one arrow had to be shot to put the enemy to flight, and the spirit of no-combat saved the lives of soldiers on both sides of the conflict.

Similar ideas are found in a book of the eighteenth century on the art of sword fighting, *Neko no myojutsu* (The Marvelous Art of a Cat), in which the secret teaching of the sword is presented through the example of a female cat and a mouse. Here, too, the result is such that a true master of the art can no longer be attacked by an enemy. Once attack has become impossible, there can be no fight, and the state of no-combat and peace begins. Of course, one must be capable of stopping or responding to an attack by an enemy whenever necessary, but the real goal of the bushi is to protect both himself and the enemy from death.

For the archer the problem presents itself in the following way: In the ancient teaching of *kyujutsu* (art of the bow), we find the concept of *aibiki*, which means roughly "shooting at each other at the same time." Aibiki presents a battlefield situation in which the archer faced a foe who placed and shot an arrow almost at the same time as himself. Whichever of the two shot inaccurately was lost—and whoever shot too late also was lost. In addition, precise, excellent technique was required to pierce the enemy's armor. Speed and precision demand self-mastery and calm at this crossroads of life and death; one had to possess a heart that had already overcome life and death.

But becoming free of the fear of death is not merely a technical problem, for even an archer who is so good that ten out of ten of his shots hits the mark can have the experience of missing a shot, perhaps just at that moment when everything depends on shooting true. Often, the cause of a miss is thoughts that disturb the archer during his shot. Even if the archer has understood that thoughts and feelings disturb his shot, he finds it difficult to turn them off.

"I don't want to think," he says to himself. "Why do thoughts still come to me while I'm shooting? Who is it that is doing this thinking? Is it I myself? I don't want to think at all, but thoughts keep coming anyway." This process, which is experienced over and over again in archery, is explained by the master of the bow in the following manner: When a person succeeds in thinking nothing, then he learns that his heart is as clear as a mirror with nothing reflected in it. But if something occurs while he is in this state, it strikes the heart as an image reflected in the mirror. If the cause of the image disappears—if the original fades away—then the reflection in the mirror disappears as well. The thoughts that disturb the archer are traces of this appearance that has been reflected in the heart. If frightening events occur, the archer must try to get at their cause without picturing their consequences; then their frightening quality will disappear. But if he fastens on an image, particularly a frightening one, then he becomes the prisoner of this image, with the result that the fear increases and multiplies.

But how does one prevent this kind of image from becoming a problem? When images seek to be reflected in the heart, let them be reflected there, and when they are ready to fade out, let them disappear. In any event, the heart must remain passive. Then it is calm and free, the heart of a master. In this state, all appearances, even the most frightening ones, become merely forms reflected in a mirror. Life and death are just such shadows in the mirror, alternating like day and night. Human beings naturally live in both the realm of life and the realm of death. If at some point death shows its image in the mirror of our heart, this shadow, too, will disappear in a new life. When the image of death reflected in the mirror is no longer capable of producing fear and there is thus also no buildup of fear, are we not then capable of transcending life and death?

In this point, all the martial arts, including the Way of the Bow, meet the teachings of Zen. If the archer, in drawing the bow, is totally absorbed in drawing, then the bow, the target, the self, and the surroundings are no longer there; nothing is there, just the sense of drawing—and a lucid, all-penetrating faculty of judgment. In this state, he can grasp with complete precision through his body that from eternity to eternity, being has remained immutable. This realization can be attained by the archer through living everyday life with a good heart and learning to coexist in harmony with people and things—and beyond that, through practicing the correct, exact, and precise art of the bow.

Kyudo practitioners have handed down this attitude to the present day; it is the attitude of those who, through practice with the bow, have experienced peace within themselves and also try to contribute toward peace in the world.

KYUDO SCHOOLS AND BRANCH SCHOOLS

A special quality of the Japanese martial arts is the existence of schools (ryu) that cultivate and preserve a particular style of the art of a given weapon. The cause of the development of such institutions was in part the fact that for a long time Japan was fragmented into many small autonomous territories. Every local prince had his own military force and needed highly qualified experts to train his warriors in the various arts of war. An outstanding fencer or archer who had survived many battles and had developed a highly evolved technique was destined to become a martial arts master and to be able to transmit his style, which was then handed down as a ryu, usually bearing its founder's name.

These schools, in addition to providing instruction, often explored and developed new techniques in the use of weapons. Thus it is easy to see how it was necessary, for military reasons alone, to keep secret from possible enemies the teachings of a given ryu with regard to techniques, strategy, and other fighting lore.

Already by the feudal period, once a student had joined a particular school, the master (*sensei*) would rank him in accordance with the level of his progress. This mode of confirming the level of a student's practice, along with titles given for special accomplishments, has been preserved up to the present day in the form of *kyu* (student) and *dan* (master) levels. The best and most mature students also received a transmission "from heart to heart" of the ultimate secrets of the art when masters made them their successors. This took place through a kind of secret teaching (*hiden* = secret tradition; *hijutsu* = secret art; *oku* = mysteries), often in the form of poems, stories, or special scrolls, which contained the quintessential teaching of the school in question with regard to both technique and spiritual training. Especially during the Tokugawa period (starting in 1600), the Zen-trained samurai were highly educated, and the texts that have been handed down from that time exhibit a high level of literary, psychological, and religious content.

If a student became a master himself, in the course of his life he would often further develop the form he had inherited; in this way he would create a new branch within his school. These modified schools bear the name *ha* or *ryuha*. For example, "Heki Ryu Insai Ha" means "Heki school, Insai branch." An overview of the various schools that taught archery on foot (referred to as *busha*, *hosha*, or *kachiyumi*, in contrast to archery on horseback, or *kisha*) is given in figure 1.3.

With the Meiji Restoration, the samurai as a class were dissolved, and their art was initially declared all but worthless.

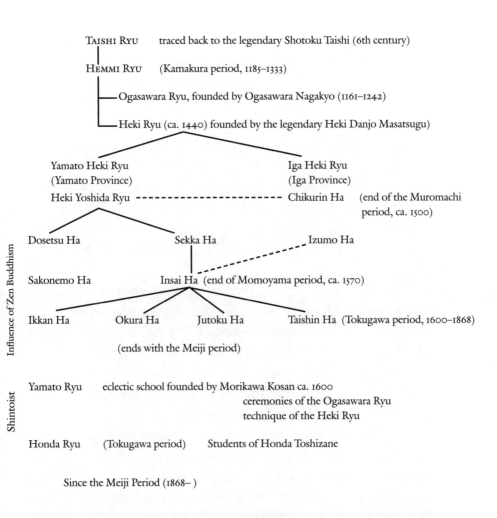
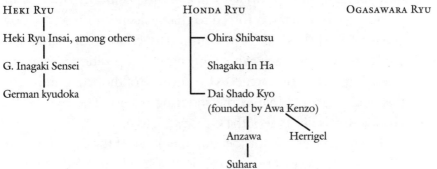

FIGURE 1.3. *Archery schools for archery on foot.*

During this period, there was a wave of adopting all manner of Western skills that went hand in hand with a neglect of ancesteral tradition, including the martial arts. This period was soon followed by one of retrospective revaluation of old values and a sense of national pride. In 1896 elder bushi assembled in Kyoto to revive "proper archery." Of the multitude of earlier schools, those existing today are the Heki Ryu (see fig. 1.4), the Ogasawara Ryu, and the Honda Ryu. In addition there are a large number of dojo that not only practice the basic style of their school but also preserve the special tradition of a particular branch school, which continues to be handed down from masters to students as in the old days.

After the Second World War, all the *kyudoka* (practitioners of kyudo) banded together in a pan-Japanese association known as Zen Nihon Kyudo Renmei, or the All-Nippon Kyudo Federation (ANKF). In spite of this movement of unification, there continue to exist—as ever in the past—the rival viewpoints of the various styles. The positive side of this is that stagnation and the creation of a generic "unity kyudo" have been prevented.

Of the remaining kyudo schools, the Ogasawara Ryu is the best known (45 percent of all kyudoka). The most conspicuous hallmark of its style is that the bow is held centered in front of the body during the preparation to shoot as well as during the raising of the bow (fig. 1.5), and it is drawn while in this position. With this approach, the bow hand is forced to change its position on the bow and is relatively less precise in form and function as compared with the Heki Ryu approach, which through a left-positioned *yugamae* (readying of the bow) achieves a secure use of the bow hand—and this is of course visible in the shooting results. The style of the Honda Ryu is like that of the Ogasawara Ryu.

Today there are about 500,000 members of the ANKF worldwide. In addition to the conception of kyudo handed down by tradition, there is increasing emphasis on sports competition and the effort to teach kyudo in the schools in the framework of sports

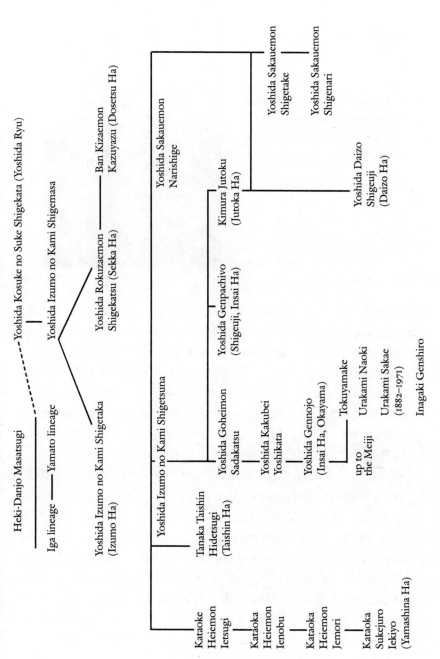

FIGURE 1.4. *Genealogy of the Heki Ryu.*

FIGURE 1.5. *Ogasawara Ryu,*
central yugamae and uchiokoshi.
Archer: H. Onuma, in
Hamburg, 1969.

education. Here we should mention the pioneer work of Inagaki Sensei, who was the first kyudoka to receive a proper professorship in the Kyudo department at the Tokyo Kyoiku Daigaku (Pedagogical University of Tokyo; today the Tsukuba Daigaku) and can be regarded as the founder of this area of specialization in Japan. In addition to being a recognition of the high personal qualifications of Inagaki Sensei, this was also favorable for the Heki Ryu, which was thus enabled to propagate its style.

Since the mid-1960s, there has been interest in kyudo outside Japan as well. An international association does not exist at the present time, but efforts to bring all kyudoka practicing in the world together in one association are under discussion. In comparison to the other budo disciplines, kyudo seems to have a rather modest number of practitioners. The Way of the Bow, seriously practiced, is difficult and demands a great deal of time if the goal of all kyudoka is to be attained, which is peace of the heart achieved through the practice of a beautiful and precise art.

弓
道

2

KYUDOJO:
THE PRACTICE HALL

IN JAPAN THE *kyudojo* (kyudo practice hall) consists of the actual *dojo*, a hall that is open on one side, and the *azuchi*, an outdoor field with a roofed target area adjoining it.

Since hardly any Japanese-style kyudojo exist in the West, where grassy fields or normal sports halls must frequently serve the kyudoka as a place of practice instead, it is a good idea to divide the areas of these practice places in accordance with Japanese tradition (fig. 2.1). This also provides the necessary level of security for archers and spectators.

THE SHOOTING AREA

Guests of honor and examiners take their place in front of the *kamiza* (literally, "divine seat"). In Japan there is frequently a small altar or a Japanese flag in the kamiza (fig. 2.2).

The area for the public should permit a view of the *mato* (targets) and leave the archers adequate room for their equipment and the preparations they need to make for shooting. The zone

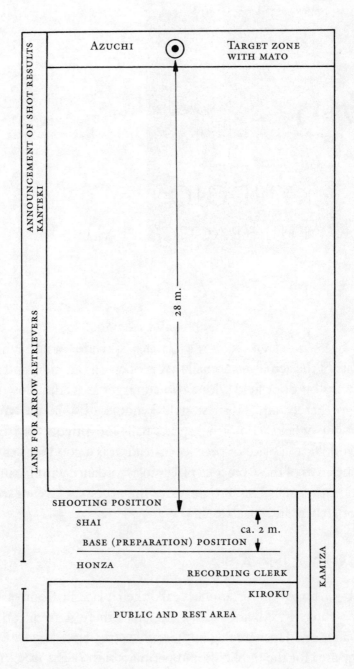

FIGURE 2.1. *The kyudojo.*

FIGURE 2.2. *Dojo no soji.*
Daily washing before practice.
In the background is the
kamiza.

for shooting immediately in front of this should be clearly defined by markings and be entered only by kyudoka about to shoot immediately. During competitions and examinations, a recording clerk (*kiroku*) sits on the boundary between the kamiza and the public area facing toward the target area.

Two lines run through the shooting area: (1) the base line (*honza*), from which the archer walks forward to shoot and to which he returns after shooting, and (2) the shooting, or center, line (*shai*), from which the distance to the target is exactly 28 meters.

After *ashibumi* (the stance), the archer's navel should be in a position directly above the center line, that is, the feet are set at about an equal distance left and right of the shai. In *enteki* (distance) shooting, the distance to the mato is 60 meters from the shai for men and 50 meters for women.

THE TARGET ZONE

To the left of the archers, a lane for the retrieval of arrows should be provided. For security reasons, a lane on the right side (from the point of view of the shooting direction) should remain an exception.

FIGURE 2.3. (Above)
Shooting hall of the kyudojo in Yudanaka (Nakano Prefecture).

FIGURE 2.4. (Left)
Waseda University Dojo.

The target zone should be set up in such a way that *all* shot arrows will surely be stopped. In a Japanese dojo this is achieved by means of an earthen embankment as well as a heavy curtain that is stretched from the eaves of the azuchi roof. Frequently a large net of fine-mesh wire, which is sure to catch high-flying arrows, is hung above the roof of the azuchi (fig. 2.4).

Since a fixed target area of this type cannot be installed in European halls, we do the best we can with straw bales or special arrow-catching nets made of nylon. The height of these nets should be at least 1.8 meters.

The distance between the individual targets should be at least 1.5 meters. The dimensions of the individual targets, their distance from the ground, the angle at which they are set up, and so on, are all ascertainable from the drawings in figure 2.5. For the standard distance, a mato of 36 centimeters in diameter is used. The *hoshimato* (star target) is usually used for competition and training sessions. The *kasumimato* (mist target) is used for ceremonies. For distance shooting (enteki), the *omato*, which is 158 centimeters in diameter, is used. The omato is stretched on a wooden frame (*matowaku*), whose dimensions are indicated in figure 2.5a–d.

In the area of the target zone is the place of the caller (*kanteki*), who shouts the results of shooting to the recording clerk.

RECORDING AND ANNOUNCEMENT OF HITS

The clerk notes the hits and misses of the archer in a shot record. In addition, the shots are summarized in four groups following the name of the archer, since a set of mato arrows is made up of four arrows.

A hit is recorded as a circle, a miss as an X. At the end, the relationship of the total number of shots to the number of hits is recorded in the following manner: If one has taken fewer than twenty shots, one writes, for example, "%₀," which means six hits out of a total of ten shots.

In competitions and examinations, shooting is done formally; that is, the next archer raises his bow in *uchiokoshi* at the moment his predecessor has shot. (See chapters 14, "Competition Forms," and 15, "Examination Forms.") The respective shot results are made known by the caller at the targets with the following calls:

1. *Atari* (hit), when the arrow hits the target
2. *Zannen* (touch; literally, "Too bad!"), when the arrow only strikes the edge of the mato or glances off the outside of it; also, when it hits the mato, but before hitting makes contact

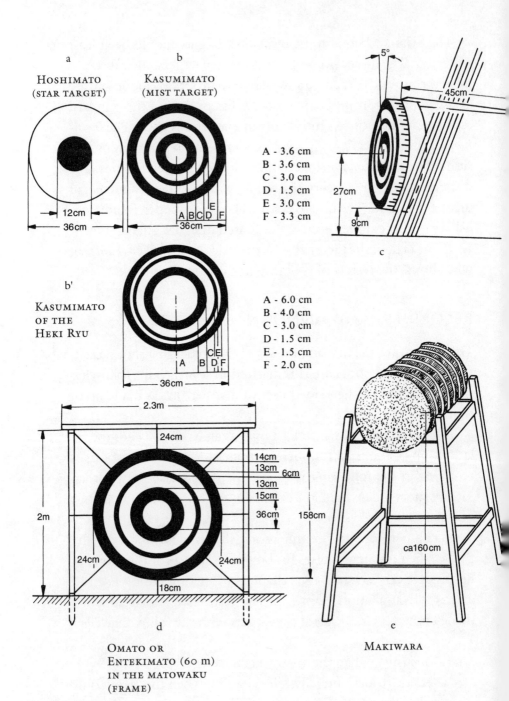

a

HOSHIMATO
(STAR TARGET)

12cm

36cm

b

KASUMIMATO
(MIST TARGET)

A B C D E F

36cm

A - 3.6 cm
B - 3.6 cm
C - 3.0 cm
D - 1.5 cm
E - 3.0 cm
F - 3.3 cm

5°

45cm

27cm

9cm

c

b'

KASUMIMATO
OF THE
HEKI RYU

A B C D E F

36cm

A - 6.0 cm
B - 4.0 cm
C - 3.0 cm
D - 1.5 cm
E - 1.5 cm
F - 2.0 cm

2.3m

24cm

2m

24cm

24cm

18cm

14cm
13cm
13cm
15cm
36cm

6cm

158cm

d

OMATO OR
ENTEKIMATO (60 m)
IN THE MATOWAKU
(FRAME)

ca160cm

e

MAKIWARA

FIGURE 2.5

with the ground and bounces up against the target. A zannen is recorded as a miss.

3. If the target is missed altogether, there is no announcement. The kanteki can also signal hits and misses by a visible gesture using the mato.
   - *In the case of hits, he holds up the front side of the target that has the target design on it for a few seconds.*
   - *In the case of misses, he holds up the white back side of the target.*

RETRIEVING THE ARROWS

Before the arrows can be retrieved from the mato area, the arrow retriever has to make sure that no more archers have nocked arrows. He stays in the arrow retrievers' lane until he has done this, then claps his hands twice and waits for the response of the archers, who call to him: *"Onegai shimasu"* ("Please do me the favor . . ."). These words allow entry into the target zone. The same is done for adjustments to the mato or their coverings. As long as any person is in the target area, no archer may continue his shot beyond the yugamae stage of the *hassetsu* (stages of shooting sequence).

The archer on whose target an adjustment has to be made calls out: *"Mato naoshimasu"* ("I adjust the mato"), or *"Ya agemasu"* ("I'm retrieving an arrow"), when, for example, an arrow is lying across the target and might be destroyed by a later hit. Then he walks in the direction of the target along the side access lane and waits until no one else is shooting, or else the other archers pause in their shooting and one of them calls out, *"Dozo"* ("Please"). Once he has fixed the mato and left the azuchi, he shouts back, *"Dozo,"* and shooting is resumed.

SHOOTING AT THE MAKIWARA

Initially the kyudo beginner shoots at a bundle of pressed rice straw, the *makiwara* (*maki* = roll, *wara* = straw; see fig. 2.5e).

The diameter of the straw target should be at least 40 centimeters and the length about 80 to 100 centimeters. The consistency of the fill must be such as to make sure arrows will catch and hold in it. Where rice straw is not available, cardboard or plastic containers very tightly stuffed with hay and closed up with fine netting (old onion sacks) have proven workable. These have about the same properties for shooting as Japanese rice straw makiwara. The makiwara must be firmly set up or hung at an optimal height for the archers. In a Japanese dojo, the makiwara are laid on massive wooden trestles. In order not to create an intrusion, the trestles are often set up in an adjacent side room and cutouts are made in the wooden wall in such a way that the makiwara just barely protrude through the wall giving onto the dojo. Suspension frames with adjustable straps have proven useful for this purpose.

Since for the lower kyu degrees, the examinations take place in front of the makiwara, the makiwara must be set up in such a way that they can be made to face the shooting coming from in front of the kamiza; this makes possible precise observation of the archers by the examiner.

OTHER DOJO EQUIPMENT

Inside a kyudojo, in the vicinity of the preparation area, there should be a rack where bows can be safely stood. In addition there must be a wooden block with a hollow in it located by the wall where a bow may be firmly set while being strung and unstrung. For storage and temporary placement of arrows, large wooden containers called *yatate* are used (fig. 2.6).

During competitions, every dojo has a large scoreboard in place on which shot results and names are written in large characters along with the official recording of the results.

Bamboo or wire rods are used to fasten the mato. These rods have their ends split in such a way that they can hold the mato by the edges.

FIGURE 2.6. *Bow stand and yatate.*

The size of the mato (36 centimeters in diameter) is delimited by a wooden ring. A few layers of newspaper are glued onto the back of the preprinted paper target sheets using ordinary paper paste (wallpaper paste). While it is still moist, the paper is fastened onto the frame with the same paste. After drying, the paper is stretched like a drumskin.

Once a dojo has reached a certain membership size, it is a good idea to keep a certain stock of materials like arrow nocks, tips, hand powder, and undergloves as the "dojo supply." Beyond that, it is desirable to help beginners by supplying rubber practice bows (and perhaps later by lending bows) and gloves for the first weeks, since acquiring one's own equipment takes some time; and moreover, the beginners' bows (ca. 9 to 10 kg pull) will soon be too weak.

DOJO ETIQUETTE

As in the other budo arts, in kyudo there are a number of rules. These rules should be regarded as an expression of courtesy toward one another and respect for the teacher, the tradition, and the dojo.

The rules presented here are the most important ones, which every kyudoka, whether in Japan or the West, should heed. These instructions for comportment are not only based on tradition, but are also fundamentally useful for the practice. A beginner in kyudo cannot immediately practice with a bow; however, it is possible to train one's attention and mindfulness when in the dojo by making an effort to behave according to kyudo etiquette and to come to the understanding that kyudo is not only practiced with a bow.

The study of kyudo means ongoing work on oneself both in the dojo and in the rest of everyday life. The goal of a balanced life cannot be reached without effort, respect for others, and patience. Some Japanese maxims indicating how this can be accomplished include: "Attentively observe nature and people, and learn," and "If your eye and mind are clear, the world is also orderly and clear." In this context, the following rules describe modes of behavior that help us to make progress toward such a goal.

1. When entering and leaving the dojo, the kyudoka bows at the entrance, first to the kamiza and then to those present.
2. When entering the dojo, the kyudoka leave their street shoes in front of the door.
3. A kyudoka arrives at the dojo in time to make all preparations—such as changing clothes, stringing the bow, and preparing the dojo—by the time the training session is to begin.
4. When lining up for the opening salutation, the most advanced members stand closest to the kamiza.
5. Before the opening salutation, all the accoutrements needed for shooting—gloves, *muneate*, *tsurumaki*, etc.—should be put down.
6. Before and after practice, one greets or takes leave of the teacher with a bow. This personal salutation should also be made when the group has performed a *rei* (ceremony) together.
7. If a teacher or an elder corrects another kyudoka, the kyudoka bows before and after being corrected and expresses thanks for the instructions and suggestions he has received.

8. When one would like to speak with the teacher, one assumes the same posture; that is, one sits before speaking if the teacher is seated, or stands if he is standing.

9. The mato furthest to the left is reserved for the teacher (*ochimato*). The succeeding mato are assigned according to dan degree or age. Beginners shoot at the mato furthest to the right.

10. In the absence of the teacher, the archer next in standing takes charge of the dojo and assumes his responsibilities for this period of time.

11. The safety rules inside the dojo (concerning order of shooting, retrieving the arrows, etc.) must be unconditionally followed.

12. All members should work actively according to their abilities in taking care of the tasks and chores that come up in the dojo, such as cleaning the floor, pasting mato, caring for the azuchi, maintaining the equipment, doing organizational work, and setting up training, competitive, and examination programs.

13. In the vicinity of the shooting zone, there should be no talking, except for corrections. For breaks, equipment maintenance, and conversations, one should always go to an area beyond the honza or into an adjoining room.

14. Eating, smoking, and drinking are allowed only in the rest area during breaks. Rules for breaks should be observed; for example, in group training, allow a break for everyone every twelve shots.

15. It is forbidden to use or even touch the equipment of another archer. Of course, the owner can make exceptions after being asked.

16. Bows, arrows, or other equipment are passed back and forth in such a way that they can immediately be taken hold of in the customary fashion.

17. The clothes worn in the dojo should be clean and correctly put on.

18. The glove and the muneate are put on and taken off in the kneeling position. An exception is when the ground might soil one's clothing.
19. Before retrieving arrows from the target area, the glove is removed.
20. It is forbidden to sight over another archer's arrow when he is shooting unless he expressly requests it. The teacher is exempted from this rule.
21. Except for the teacher, no archer should offer his opinion on a shot or make a correction unasked.

Forms of Salutation at the Beginning and End of Training Sessions

The kyudoka assemble (at the command *"Shugo"*) in the shooting zone and arrange themselves facing the kamiza in accordance with the rules. The teacher stands in front of the students, also facing the kamiza. The senior or highest-dan student gives the command *"Rei."* The teacher and students bow in unison, first to the kamiza, and then again, after the teacher has turned toward the students, to one another. The bow is performed standing, by inclining the torso slightly forward. The hands remain resting on the thighs. The head is not lowered during the bow; back and neck are also kept straight when returning to the upright position.

In Japan the following beginning and ending ceremonies for summoning and greeting various kami are also performed in front of the kamiza. Teacher and students arrange themselves facing the kamiza in accordance with the rules and, on the command *"Seiza"* (kneeling position), assume the kneeling position. Then everyone bows three times to the kamiza, raises hands as in prayer with fingers outstretched to the level of the face, then claps the hands twice. After a further bow in seiza position, everyone stands up, the teacher turns to face the students, and all perform another standing bow.

In general in the budo arts, one finds the following form of salutation. The teacher and the students take their proper places and, on the command "*Seiza*," take the kneeling position. On the command "*Mokuso*" (concentration), all place their hands together in the manner also customary during *zazen* (sitting meditation), that is, the right hand is placed palm up in front of the lower belly, the left hand rests in the same position in the right hand, and the tips of the thumbs touch each other, forming a ring. After three to five minutes, on the command "*Mokuso yame*" (end of concentration), the hands are placed once again on the thighs. On the command "*Rei*," or "*Sensei ni rei*" (greet the teacher), the students and teachers bow to each other. After the teacher has stood up, the students do likewise.

3

THE BOW

THE HISTORY OF THE BOW

As with many other cultural elements, Japan owes the bow (Japanese = *yumi*; read in the Chinese fashion = *kyu*; in antiquity also called *tarashi*) and arrow to the mainland, that is, to China or Korea. The oldest written documents that attest to the use of bow and arrow come from the first Chinese dynasty, the Hsia, approximately 1800 B.C.E. The first written documentation of the typical form of the Japanese bow is found in the *Gi Shin Toi Dan*, the Chinese historical chronicle for the province of Gi from the third century C.E. The chapter on Japan states that the Japanese bow is an asymmetrical wooden bow, made long above the grip and short below it. The oldest Japanese representation of an asymmetrical kyudo bow is found on a bronze bell, which was presented as a ritual offering in the third century C.E. The bow is a form combining the Japanese longbow with its asymmetrically placed grip and the Mongolian reflex bow. Since bows were initially made from one whole piece of wood, only a few exemplars from early times are extant. A bow that was supposed to have belonged to the legendary Empress Jingu (reigned 201–269 C.E.) is preserved in the Daianji Temple (Nara Prefecture). It is made of a round wooden branch with the bark peeled off and is about 2.2 meters long. A bow supposed to have belonged to Prince Shotoku (died 621 C.E.), also made from round branch wood, is located in the treasure chamber of the Horyuji Temple (Nara Prefecture). It is 1.95 meters long. The bows used in early times in war and for sports exercise were *marukiyumi* (round-wood bows) or *mamakiyumi* (composite—later, glued—bows: *mama* = composite; *ki* = wood; *yumi* = bow). A third type, called the *hankyu*, or half bow, was only half the length of the longbow in general use.

In early times, a simple bow made from the upper part of a tree trunk or from a branch was preferred, since, by contrast with composite bows, they were relatively insensitive to moisture, and indeed even became stronger in wet conditions and higher temperatures. Later, when the composite bow had become quite perfected, the mamakiyumi came to be preferred. In written records describing the components of bows in the Engi period (901–922), wood, leather, and horn are mentioned, but glue not at all. From this one can conclude that initially bows were held together only by wrappings and were not glued as in later times. Many writers assume that until about the middle of the twelfth century, the wrapped bow had not yet been used in war, since the most important military bow of that type, the *shigeto*, was not mentioned in the group of mamakiyumi.

In comparison to the marukiyumi, the mamakiyumi had the disadvantages of warping much more under the influence of moisture and high temperatures and becoming loose at the joints. For this reason they were initially only used for sports shooting. In order to get rid of these weaknesses, first they were coated with lacquer and the bow ends (later also the bow) were bound at several points with woven rattan (*to*) or fine-split bamboo. Finally this type of bow was perfected further as to elasticity and durability by wrapping its entirety with hemp fiber or silk cord, coating this wrapping with lacquer, and binding it at various points with woven rattan. The shigetoyumi is considered the basic type of these first composite, wrapped, and glued bows, which had thirty white rattan wrappings above the hand grip and twenty-eight below. To make this bow, one first removed the bark from two bamboo strips, carefully smoothed down the knots, and then, after having applied a coat of a mixture of flour and lacquer, tied them together with leather wrappings. The glued-on leather was then smeared with the same flour-and-lacquer mixture. Next, the entire length of the bow was wrapped with silk cord, which was also then covered with the flour-and-lacquer mixture. To prevent dust from ruining the lacquer, the bows were dried in a chest. After that, up to five more coats of pure lacquer followed; before each application, the preceding coat had to dry entirely. Places that were still rough were polished with a wet stone.

Finally, the bow received a finish coat of lacquer and its rattan wrappings. Each wrapping was about 1.8 centimeters in breadth. A thin piece of paper with an invocation to the deity Aizen Myoo was placed on the hand grip, covered by red brocade, and the whole grip was wrapped on the bias with a colored strip of leather. The color violet for the grip (*nigiri*) was exclusively reserved for the shogun. The provincial princes, who were authorized to bear a similarly worked, precious bow, had their hand grips for the most part wrapped in black leather.

There were bows similar to the shigeto, which were of simpler fabrication but made according to the same principle. The number of rattan wrappings for these varied between three and thirty. The rattan woven work on these bows was either left in its natural color or coated with lacquer at the same time as the wrapped bamboo strips. Known bow types of this sort are:

- *Motoshigeto,* a bow wrapped several times on the lower part, which was also carried by field marshals or princes. Its rattan work remained unlacquered, that is, white; the hand grip was usually wrapped with black leather.

- *Nurigometo no yumi*, a bow usually lacquered brown-black, whose rattan wrappings were lacquered at the same time as the bow. This was the most commonly used war bow.
- *Fukuzoyumi*, also called *tsukuyumi* (hook bow). This was also a wrapped and lacquered bow with seven rattan wrappings. On the spot where the arrow was placed, above the leather of the grip, a hook was affixed to rest the arrow on. This was the preferred bow for fast shooting.
- *Nuriyumi*, a lacquered bow with any number of rattan wrappings. Originally the rattan wrappings were unlacquered; later they were lacquered at the same time as the wood for the sake of greater durability.

In the course of time, gluing techniques were developed, mainly with fish glue, that made strong wrappings with rattan or cord superfluous. With time, bows were also put together out of more and more sections. The common kyudo bows of today are usually put together with seven to eight individual laminations (fig. 3.1c).

THE SHAPE OF THE BOW

An important criterion in buying a bow is its shape (*nari*). Although there are various methods of construction based on tradition and thus differing outer forms, it is nevertheless important for all bows to have their four main curves well balanced with one another. The names of the curves are:

1. *Himezori* (the princess curve)
2. *Toriuchi* (bird striker)
3. *Koshinari* (hip curve), also called *shimononari* (lower curve)
4. *Konari* (small curve); see fig. 3.1b

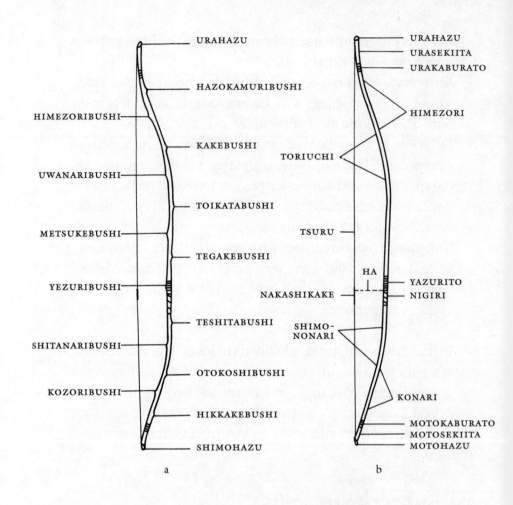

URAHAZU
HAZOKAMURIBUSHI
HIMEZORIBUSHI
KAKEBUSHI
UWANARIBUSHI
TOIKATABUSHI
METSUKEBUSHI
TEGAKEBUSHI
YEZURIBUSHI
TESHITABUSHI
SHITANARIBUSHI
OTOKOSHIBUSHI
KOZORIBUSHI
HIKKAKEBUSHI
SHIMOHAZU

a

URAHAZU
URASEKIITA
URAKABURATO
HIMEZORI
TORIUCHI
TSURU
HA
NAKASHIKAKE
YAZURITO
NIGIRI
SHIMO-
NONARI
KONARI
MOTOKABURATO
MOTOSEKIITA
MOTOHAZU

b

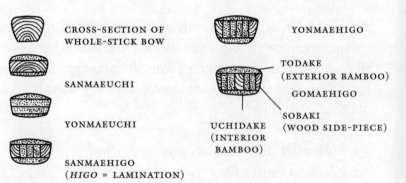

CROSS-SECTION OF
WHOLE-STICK BOW

SANMAEUCHI

YONMAEUCHI

SANMAEHIGO
(*HIGO* = LAMINATION)

YONMAEHIGO

TODAKE
(EXTERIOR BAMBOO)

GOMAEHIGO

SOBAKI
(WOOD SIDE-PIECE)

UCHIDAKE
(INTERIOR
BAMBOO)

c

FIGURE 3.1

A number of bow types still in common use today are described in the book *Yosharoku* (ca. 1675), by Yoichi Hirose. The contents of this book were transmitted to Yoichi Hirose by the founder of the Yamato Ryu, Morikawa Kosan (the first bow master to use the term *kyudo*). The bows illustrated in the book all exhibit good balance despite differences in their form, but have a different character when shot. Thus the bows with the *Satsumanari* are especially suited for sharp, penetrating shots.

The *Bishunari*, because of its slightly shortened lower end, was very well suited for enteki shooting. The *Konari* (fig. 3.2a) and *Edonari* (fig. 3.2b) are particularly suited for mato shooting and make the tenouchi a pleasure.

THE LENGTH OF THE BOW

In order to accommodate the varying body sizes of archers, bows are made in three lengths. The shortest form is called *namihoko* (standard tip). The maximum draw of a nami bow is 82–83 centimeters.

Based on the principle that in kyudo the draw length of a bow corresponds to half the height of the archer, this bow is suited for archers with a maximal height of 1.65 meters.

The next bow length is called *nobi*. This bow is longer by two *sun* (ca. 6 cm) than the nami and allows a draw of up to about 91 centimeters.

The longest bow is called *yonsunnobi*. This bow is 12 centimeters longer than the nami bow and is suited for archers who require a draw of over 95 centimeters.

Of course, each bow has its own optimal draw length. However, the three types correspond to average draw lengths and should definitely be taken into account when buying bamboo bows.

For children and very short people there is also the *sanzunzumari* bow, which is 212 centimeters, suited for a draw of less than 82 centimeters.

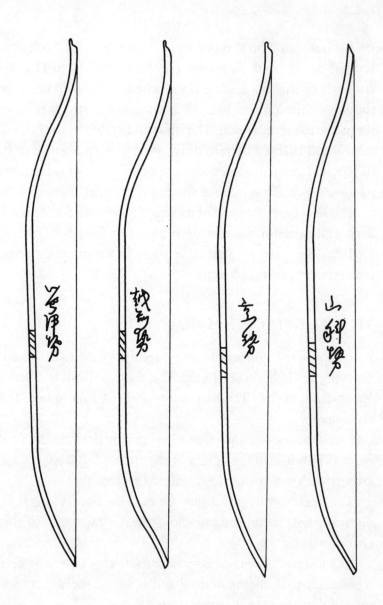

FIGURE 3.2a

NARI = FORM: *Usenari*   *Echizennari*   *Kyonari*   *Yamashinanari*

MAINLY   *Okura Ha*   *Chikurin Ha*   *Sanjusangendo*   *Yamashina Ha*
USED BY: *Yoshida Sekka Ha*   *Yoshida Ryu*

SOURCE: Yo Sha Roku by Yuichi Hirose (ca. 1675).

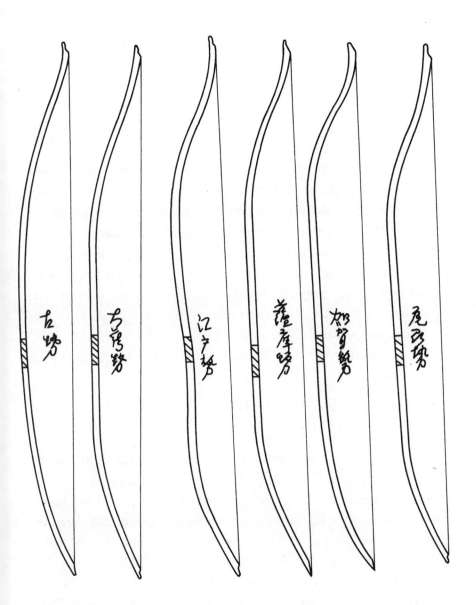

FIGURE 3.2b

Inishienari	Okuranari	Edonari	Satsumanari	Kaganari	Bishunari
Okura Ha	Yoshida Ryu Heki Ryu	Insai Ha		Yoshida Ryu	Heki Ryu

FIBERGLASS BOWS

In parallel with developments for Olympic archery, modern materials were also tried out for Japanese bows, and in the course of time they were found to be nearly as good.

Fiberglass kyudo bows are available in a variety of finishes. These bows are particularly well suited for beginning instruction, since they can be delivered in precise pull strengths, do not suffer from bad handling due to inexperience, and exhibit nearly constant shooting properties. For archers outside of Japan, a more important factor can be added—that in contrast to bamboo bows, a fiberglass bow is quite impervious to certain climatic conditions (most particularly humidity). At the present time, fiberglass bows are made in the nami and nobi lengths. Because of the greater tolerance of their material, draw lengths can be exceeded without concern.

STRINGING, EVALUATION, AND MAINTENANCE

For stringing, the upper tip of the bow is placed either in a piece of wood in the wall with a hollow in it especially prepared for this purpose, or else a second kyudoka holds the tip in her hand positioned above her shoulder. One should be careful that the point is placed in the hollow of the kyudoka's hand slightly from the right (fig. 3.3). The string is taken in the teeth, and the left hand grasps the bow just below the grip (fig. 3.4). Now the right hand pulls upward from below on the lower tip of the bow. This pull should correspond to the pull of the string, that is, it should not subject the upper tip of the bow to vertical pressure. Having preliminarily tensed the bow in this fashion, the archer takes a lunge step forward with his left foot, lays the lower tip of the bow on his left upper thigh, and loops the string onto it, after having twisted it three to seven times corresponding to how it is

FIGURES 3.3–3.5.
Stringing the bow.

wound (fig. 3.5). After stringing, the two knots in the string should be located right in the middle. At the upper tip, the coiled side of the loop should be laid to the right as viewed from the top, at the lower tip, to the left.

Next the bow should be checked over. First it should be checked for the proper depth of the bend. Measured at the grip, the distance between the grip and the string should be about 14–15 centimeters.

The bow is now held out at arm's length in such a way that the upper bow tip is lying on the floor and can freely find its point of balance at the bottom. When sighting from this point of view, it is ideal if the string is to the right of the middle line of the bow. In this case, we speak of an *iriki* bow. If the string lies to the left of the middle of the bow, we speak of a *deki* bow. The iriki form is preferred, since it favors shooting and makes the work of the bow hand easier. The slightly leftward-turning cross-section at the grip of a strung iriki bow makes it turn automatically in a counterclockwise direction when drawn—that is, in the same direction in which the bow hand is turning it. In the case of the deki bow, the direction in which the bow's cross-section turns is contrary to the direction of movement of the bow hand.

In the position described above, with the bow held at arm's length, the bow is now rotated 90 degrees, so that the archer can look at the way the wood of the bow and the string are juxtaposed (fig. 3.6). If it appears to the archer from this perspective that the bow and the string are parallel, then the form of the bow is without fault. If the bow looks too flat in its lower curvature, then the bow must be carefully pressed several times on its lower tip. If it appears too flat toward the top, then the upper point has to be carefully "massaged" in a similar fashion (fig. 3.7).

Once the bow has been properly strung, it should be fully drawn three to five times without an arrow. This drawing of the bow, called *karabiki* (*kara* = empty, *hiki* = draw), serves the archer as a warm-up exercise and also makes sure that, after being stored

FIGURE 3.6. *Assessing the form of the bow.*

FIGURE 3.7. *"Massaging" the bow.*

FIGURE 3.8. *Karabiki.*

unstretched, the string is stretched to its final length prior to shooting, and that thus the knots are also in their final position (fig. 3.8).

During maintenance and while being carried around, the strung bow is generally held by the grip. The warmth of a hand can make bamboo soft at the point where it is touched, and especially in the area above the grip, this can lead to deformations when the bow is drawn if it has not cooled off again by then.

If a bow has become too warped from being poorly stored or as a result of bad shooting technique, it must be dealt with by a specialist. A great deal of experience and knowledge of the bowmaker's art is required in order to ascertain whether a bow, in order to have the proper balance, can be trimmed or re-bent over fire, or can be corrected cold (fig. 3.9).

When the bow is no longer to be used, it is unstrung in the same way it was strung. After it is unstrung, the string is wound around the bow three to four times and held in place with a rubber band at the lower end. If the bow is not to be shot, in general it should be stored perpendicular. The place it is stored should be

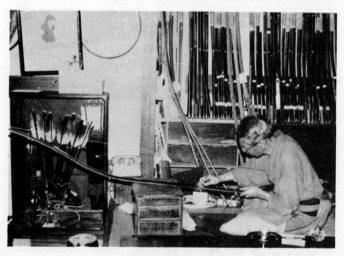

FIGURE 3.9. *Bowmaker Koyama cutting a bow. His workshop and shop are combined in the smallest possible space.*

FIGURE 3.10.
Stringing a rough form of the bow called the fujibanashi. *The glued-together laminations still have a regular, round form. Only after the bow has been strung are the iriki form and the nari obtained by bending and cutting. The first stringing requires a tremendous amount of strength; that is why there are four archers.*

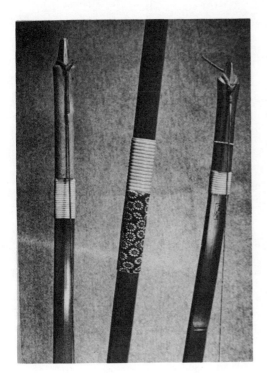

FIGURE 3.11

(Left) *Urahazu, upper tip. The winding on the knot lies to the right.*

(Center) *Nigiri (grip) and yazurito.*

(Right) *Motohazu, lower tip. The lower winding of the knot lies to the left. A rubber band is used for holding the string when the bow is not strung.*

cool, have adequate ventilation, and, most important, provide sufficient humidity. A bamboo bow should never be exposed for a long time to direct sun or central heating. Various forms of bow sheaths protect bows during storage and transport.

After use, the bow should always be kept in a light cotton sheath, into which the bow is extended from below. To protect the bow from bumps, it is a good idea to use wraparound sheaths (*yumibukuro*). This type of sheath can also be wrapped around a strung bow. For protection against rain, there are various types of plastic sheaths, in which an already wrapped bow can be placed. If the bow is to be stored for an extended period of time, it should never be stored in an airtight plastic sheath.

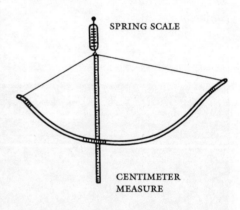

FIGURE 3.12. *Determination of the pull strength of the bow. The pull strength of a kyudo bow can be determined as illustrated. For this purpose, the bow is hung on a spring scale and drawn to the appropriate draw length* (yazuka) *for the archer in question. The question of what pull strength is optimal for a given archer must always be decided on an individual basis, since age, gender, constitution, and the length of time the archer has been practicing all come into play. However, the following average pull strengths have proven useful: beginners, 9–11 kg.; women, 12–14 kg; men, more than 14 kg.*

4

THE BOWSTRING:
Tsuru

THE HISTORY OF THE BOWSTRING

The bowstring is made by twisting hemp fibers. There were also spun strings that were much more durable, but because these were made by women, they were not very popular, since weapons that had been touched by women were considered impure and therefore unusable.

To prevent the drying out and premature splitting apart of the hemp fibers, the strings were rubbed with a blend of cedar oil and resin, which increased their durability and made them less vulnerable to moisture. Another method was to coat the strings with lacquer. For sports bows, white strings were usually preferred. War bows were by preference provided with strings coated with brown-black lacquer. The black-lacquered strings of war bows were called *nuritsuru*. Because of their particular durability, the *semenosekitsuru* were particularly renowned. These string received an additional winding along their entire length of silk thread, and then they were lacquered. Strings were usually reinforced at the nocking point to hinder rapid wear on this spot. With war bows, an almost knotlike wrapping was usually also added above the nocking point so that in the dark, or without taking his eyes off his enemy, the archer could always nock his arrow at the same level on the string. This knot is called *saguri* (feeler). *Meigen* (sounding strings) were strings that were sounded by watchmen making their rounds. These were later replaced by wooden sticks that were struck together.

To be able to replace torn strings quickly in battle, every archer kept a number of replacement strings with him. Horsemen kept their strings in a pouch called a *tsurubukuro* on the belt of their *tachi* (long sword). The present-day *tsurumaki* is derived from these round string-storage pouches.

In kyudo today, there are essentially two string types: (1) strings that are made from twisted hemp and correspond to a great extent to the historical mode, and (2) strings made from modern artificial materials. In buying a string, the main thing is to give the length of the bow. The various lengths of strings are called, like the bows, *nami*, *nobi*, and *yonsunnobi*.

In the case of strings made from natural materials, an additional distinction is drawn between summer and winter strings, and the pull strength of the bow for which the string is to be used is also taken into account.

The difference between summer and winter strings is that winter strings are more heavily treated with resin in order to prevent them from drying out in cold air. The varying pull strengths of bows is taken into account with natural strings by providing strings of different diameters.

The so-called *senbontsuru* (1,000-shot strings) made from modern plastic fibers are constructed from a material that has a stretch coefficient of nearly null. Like strings made from natural materials, they are also twisted but are coated with a thin layer of lacquer rather than resin. Senbontsuru are very durable and require little care.

In the case of strings treated with resin, it is indispensable that before and after shooting they be rubbed until warm with a string rubber (*magasune*). In this way, the resin is made to melt and coat the string. With plastic strings, this kind of treatment before and after shooting is unnecessary.

HANDLING AND CARE

With new strings, usually the lower loop is ready-made, so that the archer only has to make the upper loop and tie the upper knot to fit his bow. First the right place on the string for the knot has to be determined. To do this, one fits the lower loop onto the *motohazu* (lower bow tip) and lays the string along the inner side of the unstrung bow up to the upper tip (*urahazu*). Now one sets three fingers on the *kiritsume* (meeting point of the bamboo and the inset wooden tip) and in this way determines the point where the knot should be located, usually 5 to 6 centimeters from the kiritsume in the direction of the tip. How to make the knot can be seen from the drawings in figure 4.1. In making the first loop, one has to make sure it is not too narrow or too wide, but corresponds to the shape of the urahazu. Next one should again check whether the bow—measured at the grip—has reached the correct bend

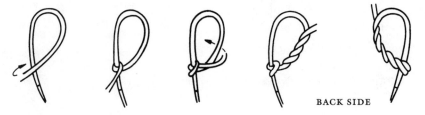

BACK SIDE

FIGURE 4.1. *Tying the knot.*

depth of 14 to 15 centimeters. In cases where the discrepancy is too great, the knot should be moved accordingly.

To reinforce the nocking point (*nakashikake*), one applies a wrapping made from hemp fibers or from the fibers of an old string that has been boiled to the point on the string across from the leather of the grip. The wrapping should be about 10 centimeters long, should begin 1 to 2 centimeters above the nocking point, and should be wound thick enough to provide a firm hold for the arrow and also enable an easy draw with the string groove of the glove. Before the glue-soaked fibers have dried, the new nakashikake is rubbed smooth and round between two pieces of wood (*doho*). After the string has been prepared in this fashion, the knots are placed precisely in the middle.

In the case of a bow where the string touches the upper part of the bow, to protect the string from wearing in this place, a wrapping like the nakashikake is also put on the string at this point (fig. 4.2).

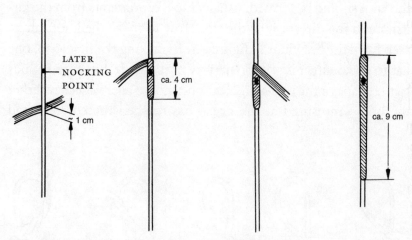

FIGURE 4.2. *Creating the nakashikake (nocking point).*

弓
道

5

THE GLOVE:
Yugake

HISTORICAL developments have left us with a multitude of different kinds of gloves. The various forms of gloves depended not on teaching methods but rather on shooting methods—that is, the purpose for which archers wanted to use the gloves.

Thus, for example, the glove for military shooting has a very soft and elastic thumb, because in former times the archer also had to be prepared to grip and wield a sword. A similar requirement existed for the horseman in *yabusame* (archery from horseback).

Since in distance shooting, very heavy bows were used, the archer often needed three or four fingers in order to be able to draw the string with his thumb (for example, the glove used in the Sanjusangendo competition).

In the Heki Ryu we use a glove that provides a shape for the thumb, the index finger, and the middle finger. The groove worked into the thumb, in which the string is caught, is the most technically important factor for the release of the shot. For normal mato shooting, the Heki Ryu prefers a groove located at a right angle to the lengthwise axis of the thumb.

This form is called *ichimonji* (sign of the number one). Beyond that, there are two other forms of groove, used by preference for long-distance shooting: the *sujikai* (deviation) form, whose string groove is at an angle of about 110 degrees from the lengthwise axis of the thumb; and the *osujikai* form, with a groove position at about 135 degrees from the lengthwise thumb axis.

The glove's individual parts and their names can be seen in figure 5.1.

To protect the glove from perspiration and moisture, a cotton underglove is always worn during shooting (fig. 5.2). To prevent the glove from getting smooth and slippery, the insides of the fingers of the glove (the surfaces that touch each other between the thumb, index, and middle fingers) are never touched with the

FIGURE 5.1. *Yugake (kyudo glove). (a) Boshi: tip of thumb. (b) Koshi: "hip." (c) Hikae: wrist support. (d) Daikawa: large leather piece. (e) Hinerikawa: release leather piece. (f) Yubi: finger. (g) Haragawa: "belly" leather piece. (h) Tsurumakura: string cushion = string groove. (i) Kohimo: small tie. (j) O: large strap. (k) Mon: family crest.*

FIGURE 5.2. *A cotton underglove is always worn during shooting.*

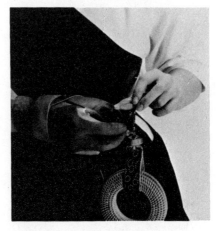

FIGURE 5.3

fingers. To obtain the optimal level of friction on these contacting surfaces of the three fingers (which should not become sticky either), the *boshi* (tip of the thumb) and the corresponding contacting surfaces on the ring and middle fingers are powdered with *giriko* (a rosin mixture) and made slightly tacky with a rubbing movement on the leather in the direction of the fingertips. This movement makes a grating sound (*giri*), (fig. 5.3).

In tying the glove, the thinner part of the leather strap (*kohimo*) is wound around the wrist immediately below the wrist bone. While doing this, the hand is held as it is normally held during shooting (fig. 5.4). The binding should not be too tightly wound around the glove. The end is made into a five-cornered knot on the inner side (fig 5.5).

FIGURES 5.4 AND 5.5. *Putting on the glove.*

In buying a glove, an archer can choose from among various models of ready-made gloves or may decide on a glove custom-made for his own hand. Custom-made gloves are of course more expensive than ready-made. However, the price is mainly determined by the quality of leather that is used. Although gloves from goatskin or pigskin skiver are cheap, because of the structure of the leather, they have only a short life. The leather best suited for the gloves is deer or antelope hide. Leather from the middle of the back of the hides has the best quality for glove manufacture. In contrast to leather from, for example, the side parts of the hide, it has uniform qualities of strength and structure. A further price factor is embroidery and decoration on the glove. Having, say, a family coat of arms worked onto the back of the glove raises the price by about 20 percent.

In buying a glove, the main thing to make sure of is that the thumb and the arch between the thumb and index finger have a good and comfortable fit. In the case of ready-made gloves, a frequent problem is that the fingers are too long. But this is not a disadvantage. The most important thing is that the diameter of the glove finger should fit the circumference of the user's finger.

New gloves are often very rigid. They have to be broken in by shooting, and it is a good idea before and after shooting to massage the area around the string groove and the reinforced area that lies against the inside of the arm (*hikae*) into their typical S-form so they will better accommodate the form of the hand.

It is also advisable during the first month of use not to pull the binding of the glove to maximum tightness, because in this way lightly glued or sewn seams might be overstressed and tear, since the glove is still too inelastic.

弓
道

6

ARROWS:
YA

Arrows were acquired by Japan from China at the same time as bows. It is said that willow wood was originally used, since its lightness and suppleness made it good for arrow shafts. To keep the dried-out wood from breaking, it was customary to rub it with oil. Along with willow, bamboo was also used. Arrowheads were made from iron or copper, finished with bamboo, horn, or bone. Many arrows from early times have been preserved, along with bows, in the treasure chambers of the temples of Horyuji and Daianji. These are certainly the oldest extant arrows. They are about 90 centimeters in length and no longer have any feathers; however, traces at the point of attachment allow us to tell that they formerly had two, three, or four feathers.

They are:

- *Togariya*: arrows with spear-shaped heads, frequently provided with barbs (*watakuri* = gut rippers).
- *Yatsumekabura* and *mutsumekabura*: arrows with a ball of horn

(*kabura*) set in between the shaft and the head with 8 (*yatsu*) or 6 (=*mutsu*) holes (*me* = eyes) in it.

- *Takeyajiri*: arrows with bamboo heads.
- *Kururiya*: arrows with large, thick heads made from light wood.

A comparison between these early types of arrows with arrows that were in use later, and then again with the arrows of today, shows that this weapon has been subject only to very slight changes. The normal length for an arrow from the Middle Ages up to modern times has been given as three *shaku*, about 90 centimeters (1 shaku = 32 cm = 10 sun = 100 *bu*). The length of individual arrows depends on the height of the archer; it corresponds to half his height plus roughly 5 to 8 centimeters. Another unit of measure was the *soku*, which corresponds to the size of the closed fist, not including the thumb. Fourteen to fifteen of the archer's soku yielded the length of the arrow. The style of fabrication of the shaft (*no*), the lower end of the arrow (*hazu*), the head (*ne*) and the attached feathers (*ha*) gave the arrows their names.

THE SHAFT (NO)

Two-year-old bamboo is used almost exclusively for the shaft. Three-year-old bamboo is considered no longer suitable for arrows. The length of the shaft is between 80 centimeters and 1 meter. The number of rings in the bamboo is not fixed, but for the most part there are four. Each ring has a special name, or even different names depending on whether the arrow in question is a war arrow or a sports arrow (fig. 6.1a). By its natural color, the bamboo shaft stripped of its bark was white or brown, if it was roasted or browned over a straw fire in order to make it harder and less flexible. It was also customary to coat arrows with black or red lacquer in order to protect them from moisture. The common arrow shafts and their names were as follows:

- *Shirano:* white, natural-colored shaft
- *Kogashino* or *aburino:* roasted, brown shaft
- *Suyaki:* burnt, brownish arrow, used in competition shooting
- *Sawashino:* steamed black-lacquered arrow
- *Kawame norinono:* a shaft lacquered to resemble bamboo bark
- *Nogoinono:* red-lacquered shaft
- *Fushikage:* shaft with shiny black lacquer on the bamboo rings and ring shadows, that is, the places from which the bamboo leaves were broken.

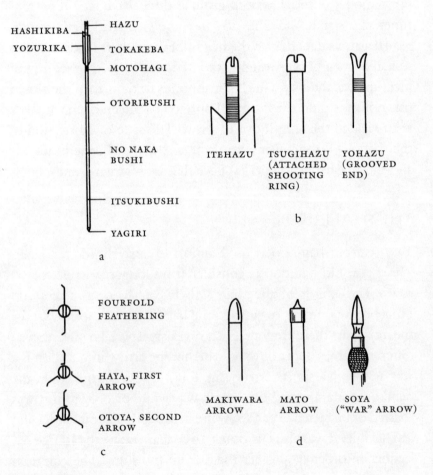

FIGURE 6.1

The procedure for making the *matoya* (mato arrows) of today runs something like this: After the bamboo has been cut, it is dried for six to eight months. During this time the shaft shrinks in length and thickness, and initially it is not straight. The first step in working it is called *neru* (forming). During neru, the arrow is moved back and forth over a charcoal fire and roughly formed with a notched piece of wood that serves as a lever for straightening it. After this, the arrow shaft is almost straight and is now roughly worked on the surface with a drawknife. This step in the work is called *aradame* (rough correction). In the following *nakadame* (intermediate, further correction), the arrow is straightened over a fire once more and has its surface shaved again (fig. 6.2). Finally comes the *ishiarai* (*ishi* = stone, *arai* = washing), a procedure in which the arrow is pulled through an oval stone in which two grooves have been driven. Sand is used here as an abrasive. Being pulled back and forth through the stone grooves finally gives the shaft a smooth and even surface. Now that the shaft has been smoothed, hardened, and straightened in this manner, we come to the final step, in which the arrow is either oiled or lacquered. An arrow shaft made in this way is called *yanochiku*, or treated bamboo.

Three types of yanochiku are distinguished:

1. *Ichimonji* (number-one sign). The name of this type of arrow comes from the sign for the number one, which in Japan is a straight stroke. For the arrow shaft, this means that its diameter remains unchanged throughout its entire length. The ichimonji is the standard arrow.
2. *Mugitsubo* (grain of wheat). This arrow has its greatest diameter in the middle and tapers toward the two ends; hence the name "grain of wheat." Arrows with this sort of cross-section require a good tsunomi to ensure that their center of gravity remains truly in the middle while in flight. The mugitsubo is especially well suited for enteki shooting.

FIGURE 6.2. *Arrowmaker straightening a bamboo shaft with the help of a brazier* (lower left) *and a lever.*

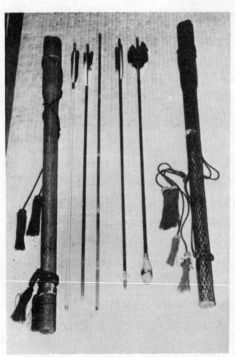

FIG. 6.3. (Left to right) *woven bamboo yazutsu, aluminum arrow, matoya, makiwara arrow, togariya for koshiya, hikimeya, yazutsu of woven lacquered paper.*

3. *Suginari* (cedar-shaped). This arrow shaft has a conical form when looked at from the side. The diameter is least near the feathers and greatest near the point. These arrows are very well suited for target shooting, since they are heaviest at the point. In addition, these arrows can be used for a very long time, since the forward part of the arrow that ends up sticking in the earth gradually gets worn down, so that little by little one ends up with an ichimonji.

Bamboo arrows have gotten their form by being dried and worked over heat. But they can also lose their form due to both of these elements. Too much moisture or blazing sun damages them over a long period of time and makes them warp. However, if an archer has the necessary experience and the appropriate tool, if he handles it properly, he can restraighten a crooked arrow over an open gas flame. In countries where the humidity of the air may be significantly less than it is in Japan, since bamboo reacts with particular sensitivity to this condition, it may be a good idea to rub arrow shafts from time to time with a nonresinous oil such as clove oil, especially around the ring shadows, to prevent them from drying out.

NOCKS (HAZU)

In order to secure the arrow firmly on the string, on its end there is a notch from 2 to 5 millimeters in depth. The variation in this dimension depends on the type of arrow. Three main types of hazu (fig. 6.1b) are distinguished.

1. *Tsugihazu* is the attached end, which in earlier times was a notched bamboo ring set onto the end of the arrow. The type with attached ends was common in ancient times for practice arrows, arrows for shooting at targets (matoya), and sports arrows (*jindo*).

2. *Yohazu* is the grooved end, which came to be used for war arrows (*soya*, togariya, etc.). The notch was cut directly into the bamboo shaft.

3. *Itehazu* is the shooting end, made out of an attached piece of horn, and it has been preferred for practical reasons in modern times owing to its greater durability and its smaller circumference. Today's mato arrows are equipped exclusively with this type of nock.

WRAPPINGS

Wrappings are put on the arrow in various places; in some cases they serve to fasten the feathers and the points, and in others to strengthen the shaft itself. Their names indicate the purpose they are meant to serve or the places on the arrow where they are placed.

- *Urahagi:* the top wrapping, about 1.3 centimeters wide, which fastens the quill of the feather above the feather onto the shaft.
- *Motohagi:* the bottom wrapping, about 1.8 centimeters wide, which holds the quill of the feather below the feather.
- *Kutsumaki:* the shoe wrapping, also called *yatsukamai* (arrowbag wrapping), about 3 to 5 centimeters wide, which was wrapped around the tip of the shaft to keep it from bursting.
- *Kanemaki:* the metal binding for holding in place the long arrowhead tang that is driven into the shaft and also for preventing the upper end of the bamboo from bursting.
- *Netamaki:* a bulging, often bell-shaped wrapping, intended for the same purpose as the kanemaki
- *Kaburamaki:* a similar ball-shaped wrapping, which was mostly used with *karimata*, arrows with forked heads.

The materials used for the wrapping are evident from their names:

- *Itohagi:* thread wrapping. This wrapping is done with white or colored silk cord. Specific colors were reserved for the use of the shogun and the daimyo (higher nobles).
- *Kamihagi:* paper wrapping. A wrapping made with very durable and firm, thinly rolled paper.
- *Kabahagi:* bark wrapping. This wrapping is made with the bark of the cherry tree.
- *Urushihagi:* wrappings that are coated with lacquer.

FEATHERS

Valuable feathers were rarely used for arrows that were to be shot once, but were used for sport and hunting arrows that could be retrieved. For war arrows (soya), the choice was raptor feathers, because they are sturdy and tough. The feathers of the hawk, the harrier, the crane, and the wild goose were popular, but raven and chicken feathers were also used. Never, on the other hand, were feathers of the eagle owl used, since this bird was considered an evil omen in Japan. The best feathers are the outside tail feathers of the eagle. Since they are especially tough, they are also called *ishiuchi*, which means "rock striker," because this feather is so hard it can withstand striking a rock. Of almost equal quality are the outside wing feathers. Following next in quality are the lower middle feathers of the tail and the other wing feathers. All other feathers are often too soft and not suitable for fletching arrows. Since many raptors are nearly extinct, fletching made from eagle feathers, for example, in matching colors, is almost unaffordable.

For the fletching, feathers of about 14 centimeters in length are needed. They are either trimmed or left in their natural form and, as already mentioned, with silk-thread wrapping, fastened onto the arrow shaft by their split quill. In earlier times, certain feathers were attached to the shaft by the whole quill.

Arrows are fletched with three, four, and sometimes only two feathers. Generally three feathers are used for sports arrows.

Feathers are distinguished according to their color and markings:

- *Torafu:* striped feathers
- *Motoshiro:* feathers that are white at the root
- *Tsumaguro:* black-edged feathers
- *Hoshikirifu:* star-spotted feathers
- *Itofu:* feathers with threadlike markings

To achieve the most uniform possible markings on all the arrows of a set, among other things, people have tried combining feathers, that is, gluing feathers of different colors on the same quill to make them look like one feather. It was hoped in this way to attain the desired decorative effect. Such markings also occur naturally in nature but are rarely to be found in twelvefold uniformity. Popular markings, among others, were:

- *Kiriu:* feathers with a white band in the middle
- *Nakaguro:* feathers that were black in the middle
- *Usobyo:* feathers speckled at the root

HAYA AND OTOYA (FIG. 6.1C)

In kyudo today, a set of matoya is composed of four arrows, two *haya* ("arrow A") and two *otoya* ("arrow B"). The difference between these two kinds of arrows lies in the way in which the feather is glued to the shaft and how it is curved at the end (fig.6.1c).

In the haya, the glued-on part of the feather quill is toward the archer as he nocks the arrow onto the bowstring. If one looks at the arrow from the nock end, the feathers are arched to the left.

In the otoya, the feather quill is glued on the side not visible to the archer. Looked at from the nock, the feathers are curved to the right.

The reason for the different mode of attachment and arrangement of the feathers is that, in the case of two arrows shot theoretically under the same conditions, because of the slight variation in the feather, the second arrow will never strike the same point as the first arrow and thus will not damage its valuable shaft and feathers.

In ceremonies and competitions, the haya is always shot first and then the otoya. The haya is preferred as the first, more perfect arrow, because when it is viewed from the direction of the kamiza, it does not allow a view of the glued-on quills of the feathers.

To keep valuable arrows from being damaged by negligence, the feathers also have to be checked from time to time. If a feather has become loose from the shaft, it can be fastened again with a drop of glue. To make sure of the contact with the shaft, it is a good idea to pull a thin thread down through the vane of the feather and fasten the quill to the arrow with that. If the feather has become ruffled so that the individual barbs stand apart from each other, it is possible to resmooth such a feather over steam. After drying, the individual barbules on the barbs will fit back into each other, and the feather will again be smooth. Arrows should generally be kept in a closed quiver. It is a good idea to put in some moth crystals, since moths and mites like to attack feathers.

If a feather has been completely destroyed, one has to loosen the wrapping on the shaft and replace the whole feather. In that case it is a good idea to change all three feathers; otherwise the inner balance of the arrow may be thrown off.

Another question related to balance is whether to use wide or narrow feathers. For normal mato shooting, wide feathers are preferred, whereas for enteki shooting, narrow feathers are used.

SIGNATURE

The name of the owner is often marked on arrows. This is done with ink or lacquer, by burning in the letters, or by scratching them in with a knife. These markings are either made between the two wrappings on the nock or inconspicuously between the feathers. In earlier times, samurai used to add the names of their feudal lords as well as their title and province to the signatures, so that every warrior could tell by whom he was being attacked.

FIG. 6.4. Dog Hunt, *wall screen painting, end of the 16th century, Tokyo National Museum.*

An exception in the matter of signatures—out of courtesy—was the markings on sports arrows used in dog hunting (*inuoi*; fig. 6.4). These arrows were marked with special but anonymous signs, never with the owner's name, since it often happened in the fields where the hunts were taking place that horses stepped on the arrows, and it would have been regarded as an indignity to have the name stepped on in this manner.

ARROWHEADS

The heads (ne) were made of iron, horn, wood, and, in ancient times, also copper. For war arrows, only iron arrowheads were used, since these were capable of piercing armor. In competitive shooting in historical times, heads of wood and horn were preferred, while for dog hunting and sports arrows, all types of heads have been used.

The lengths of arrowheads vary between 3 and 5 centimeters. A rare but highly valued type of head of 18 to 20 centimeters in length is called *tametomonoya*, after the renowned twelfth-century archer Tametomo. Individual exemplars of this type of arrowhead are still preserved in temples.

The names of a few arrowsmiths are known; however, arrowheads were not only made by specialists, but often also by master armorers and swordsmiths. There are few cases of signed arrowheads.

Different forms of arrowheads were required for different purposes. Some were suited, for example, for piercing armor, splitting shields, or producing flesh wounds, or for use in close combat or for indirect shots against attacking cavalry (see also fig. 7.2).

The names of the individual types of heads often indicate the form, less often the purpose:

Karimata: forked arrowheads in the form of the feet of a wild goose
Haiwo: fly-tail-shaped heads, a variation of karimata
Hokoya: spear-shaped heads, with the following subcategories:
- *Torijita:* bird-tongue shaped
- *Tatewari:* chisel-shaped in the form of a two-edged sword point; used as a shield splitter
- *Togariya:* spear-shaped arrowheads
- *Watakuri:* gut-ripping arrowheads with barbs
Marune: massive, completely round arrowheads
Nomine: chisel-shaped arrowheads

These basic forms were produced in a great variety of subforms over the course of time; these carry names that suggest what they resemble—for example, willow leaf (*yanagiba*), triangle (*sankaku*), and flying buzzard (*tobine*).

Frequently we find arrowheads—especially of the *kaburaya* type and the broad, turnip-shaped *hirane*—that have multiple perforations, in the form of geometrical figures and family coats of arms, but also written characters. Very frequently we find heart-shaped perforations. They are called *hoshonotama* (flaming pearl) or also *inome*, the never-flickering eye of the wild boar (fig 7.2). If arrow-heads have perforations depicting written characters, these indicate either clan names, especially in the case of the ornamental arrows of provincial princes, or else phrases of prayer or the names of deities. In the last case, it is presumed that these are votive arrows, which were offered to the war gods by placing them in temples.

There are various hypotheses concerning the richly orna-mented kaburaya. According to one, this arrow was the last arrow in the possession of a samurai. Only at the moment a battle was considered lost would he have shot this arrow. After the leader had shot this principal arrow, defeat was acknowledged, and only *sep-puku* (ritual suicide by cutting open the bowel) remained. Another interpretation is that there was a *tainoya*, a base arrow that was used in quivers in which the arrows rested on the bottom, that is, were not held by a bamboo framework laid over them that kept them together or upright. This arrow was fastened to the outside of the quiver, in a sense as a corner post that, together with leather loops, supported the other arrows. It is said of the tainoya that it was never shot but accompanied its bearer into the beyond.

For sport and competitive shooting, as well as for the hunt, blunt arrows were often needed. *Itazuki* were round, square, or flat arrowheads of wood or horn that were tipped with a thin metal cap.

Nail-shaped arrowheads made of iron were called *byone*, and square ones of the same metal were called *jotaku*. These were in-tended to stun but not kill animals.

In present-day kyudo, different arrowheads are used for maki-wara arrows than for matoya. In order to damage the straw in the bale as little as possible, rounded iron or horn tips are used (fig. 6.1d).

For mato arrows, attached heads made of iron are used. On aluminum arrows, either attached iron heads or cone-shaped points are used; these are directly attached to a short shaft set into the main arrow shaft.

TYPES OF ARROWS

War Arrows

War arrows were often called soya or *seisen*, but also *shuraya* (arrow for the fighting ground) or *senjonoya* (arrow for the battlefield). These had a black lacquer bamboo shaft and a grooved end (yohazu), were usually fitted with falcon feathers, and had a lacquer-coated wrapping on the end of the shaft, the *netamaki*. The arrowheads were mostly spear-shaped.

A *hitokoshi no soya* was a set of twenty-five, twenty, or sixteen war arrows, which the archer carried with him in a quiver. Every quiver with more than twenty arrows contained the so-called *uwasashi* (top arrow) and *nakasashi* (middle arrow). The uwasashi had the form of a kaburaya, the nakasashi that of a togariya.

Togariya was a war arrow with a lance-shaped head, which was fitted out like the soya (fig. 6.3).

Watakuri, the gut ripper, was a kind of togariya with a spear-shaped head, which was provided with long sharp barbs. This arrow is said to have been the arrow of choice for blood vengeance.

Kaburaya (from *kabura* = turnip) is an arrow with a bell-shaped or ball-shaped head made out of hard wood or horn. The holes made in the heads of these arrows caused the arrows to give out a whistling, wailing sound when shot. These whistling heads had points in the form of karimata or ganmata attached to them, iron points in the form of the foot of a wild goose, although sometimes other kinds of points were used.

Arrows for Target and Competitive Shooting

Tsunogi was the name for a practice arrow used to shoot at straw-bale targets. It had an attached nock; the head was commonly made of horn.

Botsunogi was the name of an arrow that was a tsunogi without feathers. It is more or less the ancestor of the arrow used nowadays to shoot at makiwara.

Matoya, the historic arrow for target shooting, initially had a natural-colored shaft but later was burned brown or black, or else was colored black, brown, or red by lacquering. The attached nock was fastened on with a wrapping of paper fibers. For fletching, eagle feathers (*maha* = genuine feather) or feathers of other birds were used, but never feathers of the hawk, stork, or eagle owl. Originally the feathers were fastened on with bark wrappings, later also with wrappings of paper fiber. The point was formed of an arrowhead (*itazuki*) that was fashioned of paper wrapping on the end of the shaft. A thin metal cap was fitted over this point.

The form and structure of the mato arrow has remained the same up to the present day. The only differences are that silk thread is used to fasten the feathers on, and the metal point is now placed directly on the bamboo shaft.

Sashiya (piercing arrows) and *kururiya* were two arrow types preferred for shooting long distance. The shafts and the fletching were kept relatively simple. The heads were made of wood.

Hunting and Sports Arrows

Noya (also called *shishiya*) was a hunting arrow that was very similar to the war arrow; it was the arrow of choice for bear and stag hunting.

Karimata was a hunting arrow with a forked iron point, a kind of kaburaya with thick, ball-shaped wrapping on the head.

Kururiya was an arrow that had a kabura or bulge that was hollowed out inside so that, when used for hunting waterfowl, the arrow would float on water. Small forked iron heads were used.

Jindo is literally translated as "head of a god." This was an arrow that ended in a kabura. The types principally used for hunting dog were *kazujindo* (multiple jindo) and *hitotejindo* (simple jindo). Attached heads are rare on these arrows. The feathers were often attached to the shaft in their natural form.

Shime (also called *naruya*) is an arrow that resembles the jindo, which is supposed to have been used for hunting stag, not to kill the animal but rather to stun it.

Special Types

Hikimenoya (toad-eye arrow) has an egg-shaped bulge roughly 10 to 20 centimeters in length made from bamboo or horn and has several holes in the head. As air enters the head during the shot, the holes produce, as with the kabura, a whistling, screeching noise. The inuoi hikime was used for dog hunting, the *kasakake* hikime as a signal in competitions, and the sanya no hikime to drive away evil spirits (fig. 6.3).

Hiya (fire or flame arrow) was used as early as the twelfth century during the clan war of the Genji against the Heike to destroy fortresses and castles. The hiya is said to have had a kabura that was filled with inflammable material. The shaft was made of iron, which was wrapped with easily inflammable fabric; the arrow was often given stability through the use of wooden "feathers," which were also impregnated with inflammable substances (oil, ignition powder, tar). The hiya was shot not only by archers but also by crossbow-like catapults, whose range is said to have been about 270 meters.

Two types of poison arrows were known in Japan: (1) *dokuya*, the head of which was smeared with the juice of the monk's hood plant; and (2) *totokinoya*, an arrow with a poisoned feather shaft.

In the literature the Japanese mention that they themselves never used these arrows, but this type of arrow was utilized by "foreigners." According to the code of bushido, poisoned weapons were considered dishonorable. However, a special group of spies (*ninja*) demonstrably also used poison as a means in fighting.

7

QUIVERS

For storage and transport of their arrows, kyudoka use *yazutsu* (quiver tubes). These usually consist of a slender cardboard tube, which widens at the level of the fletching and closes with a cap. The tube can be lacquered or, for decoration, wrapped with a variety of materials such as cherry-tree bark, rattan, woven bamboo, or lacquered paper cord (fig. 6.3).

Historical quivers have little in common with arrow storage containers used by present-day kyudoka. Only in the case of military shooting (*kazuya, koshiya*) and yabusame is a historical type of quiver, the *ebira*, still in use. Although in early China, there were also quivers from which the arrows must have been pulled vertically over the shoulder, the Mongolian shooting technique required that the arrow be laid on the bow from the right, and thus the Chinese (the Lolo tribe of the upper Yangtse Kiang) developed quiver types that made it possible to fit the arrow to the bow quickly with a horizontal movement. Probably the *utsubo* (fig. 7.1) was derived from the top-opening quiver (*yugi*). With this type of quiver, the arrows also stand with their points downward in a

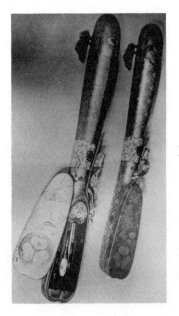

FIG. 7.1. *Utsubo.*

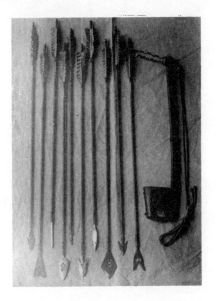

FIGURE 7.2. *Open quiver of the shiko type with various arrows.* (Left to right) *watakuri; ryokai with inome; togariya; watakushi with cherry blossoms; sankaku watakuri with inome; rinzetsu; sashiya with blossoms; watakuri; karimata with fan.*

closed container, the feathers are protected, and the archer can take hold of the arrow directly by the head, pull it out of the quiver from below, and thus load it quickly. An intermediate form is the *shiko*, an open quiver that can be hung on the belt from a hook especially made for it (fig. 7.2).

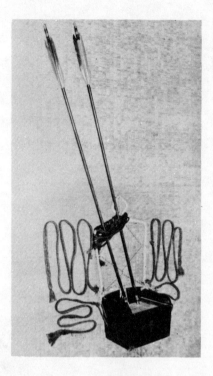

FIGURE 7.3. *Ebira.*

The quivers most often used by samurai up to quite recent times were the ebira (fig. 7.3).

Despite many variants, the following structural elements are always found: The base element is a wooden box, covered with hide on the back side, in which there is a gridlike framework (*yanagui*) to receive the arrowheads. A frame set on the back of this and special coils of cording support and hold the arrow shafts. The quiver is tied onto the right hip and holds up to forty arrows.

8

弓道

DRESS

BASICALLY, KYUDO CAN be practiced in any exercise clothing; that is, it can also be practiced in normal Western sportswear or leisure dress. But if the archer practices that way, he has to be sure that he is not wearing garments that are too confining. In particular, diaphragmatic breathing should not be hindered, and the ability to lift the arms to draw the bow must be unrestricted. If one shoots in "civvies," both men and women must wear a muneate (breast protector), so that the bowstring will not be obstructed by their clothing in its forward movement during the hanare.

The traditional clothing for the kyudoka consists of a shirt (*gi*), skirtlike trousers (*hakama*), a broad sash (*obi*), and socks (*tabi*).

The men's garments are made somewhat differently from the women's clothing. The women's hakama has no *hakama no kushita* (trapezoid-shaped back piece); instead of this, the rear waistband has a somewhat broader form. As for the gi, there are openings under the armpits for better ventilation in the men's but

1. *The beginning end (A) of the obi is placed on the right half of the back, and the other end (E) is wrapped around the hips three to four times. The layers should be precisely on top of one another.*

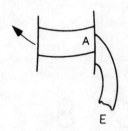

2. *The beginning end (A) is pulled out and up, just about to the middle of the back. The end is doubled over inward, producing an end piece about 40 cm in length.*

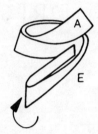

3. *The beginning of the obi is stuck under the end, and the end is pulled upward under the descending piece of the beginning.*

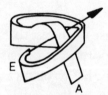

4. *The cross thus formed is pulled tight.*

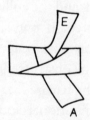

5. *And the upper part is rolled.*

FIGURE 8.1. *Tying the Obi.*

6. At the middle of the belt, the rolled end is now wrapped in the beginning end; that is, the beginning is brought over the rolled end and then tucked around the layers of belt already circling the body.

7. The back piece of the hakama is then placed on top of the cushion formed in this manner.

not in the women's. The women's belt is simpler and shorter than the men's, and usually more colorful.

For ceremonial shooting (*sharei*), instead of the white gi, a large kimono with wide sleeves and the accompanying light underkimono (*monpuku*) are worn. Since the wide sleeves would obstruct the forward movement of the bowstring, when wearing the large kimono, women use a white cord (*tasuki*), with which both sleeves are tied back. Men solve the problem by removing the left arm from the sleeve before shooting.

Women wear a breast protector, or muneate, for every shooting form.

First, the kyudoka puts on the gi and ties the strings together on the inside and the outside in such a way that the upper part ends up lying from left to right. Then the sash is put on over the jacket in such a way that the upper edge lies more or less on the hipbones. The different ways of tying the sash for men and women can be seen in figures 8.1–8.3. In any case, the sash should not be too tight, since otherwise it obstructs breathing.

Before putting on the hakama, as the final piece of clothing to be donned, one pulls the back side of the jacket flat, so that any wrinkles that might develop will be on the sides under the arms. With the hakama, first the two front ties are fastened. They are drawn to the back, parallel to but slightly below the upper edge of the sash; they are crossed behind and drawn again to the front, now along the lower edge of the sash. The point where the ties cross should be below the navel, which corresponds approximately to the lower edge of the obi. Then the two ends are once more drawn to the back along the lower edge of the sash and tied there with a knot and bow.

Now the trapezoidal back piece of the hakama is placed over the knot of the sash, and the two rear ties are drawn to the front to the crossing point below the navel and there fastened to the

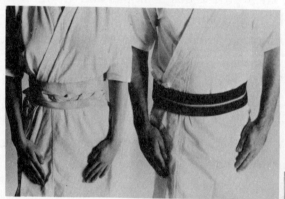

FIGURES 8.2 AND 8.3. *The woman's and man's obis in place (front and rear views).*

front ties with a knot. The loose ends can be either stuck sideways under the sash or made into a nice bow or knot.

The fastening of the women's hakama is done in essentially the same way, except that here—because the sash is narrower and is at the waistline—the ties are not crossed so that they lie apart, but rather so that all of them lie on top of one another. The rear ties of the women's hakama are tied with a knot and bow at the right hip.

A special point about taking measurements should be mentioned: For the hakama, the size is based on the measurement in centimeters from the hipbone to the instep; for the tabi, the measurement is from the heel to the big toe.

9

ACCESSORIES

Along with the bow, arrows, and glove, kyudoka carry with them in lacquer-ornamented leather pouches a number of things that are useful for care and maintenance.

In order not to disturb other archers during their practice, it is indispensable to have a certain number of replacement parts on hand at all times. This is especially true for kyudoka who are representing their clubs at competitions. The following should be available:

1. *Replacement bowstrings*, which already have the reinforcement in place. The reinforcement should always be placed at the right level at the nocking point. In certain cases it is a good idea to put an additional wrapping slightly below the upper knot in case the bowstring (despite the proper bend depth of 14 to 15 cm measured at the grip) grazes the bow. The bowstrings, fully prepared for the bow with wrappings and knots, are kept rolled up, since otherwise they break easily. This is especially true for the resin-treated natural strings; but strings made from plastic get weak spots and worn areas if they are not properly protected

when stored. In rolling the strings, one should slightly twist them in the direction in which they are wound.

2. *Tsurumaki* (string-roll storage rings). There are rings for storing the prepared strings, made in various ways: from lacquered paper, rattan, or also plastic. Often a small flask is attached to this with a leather loop (fig. 5.3).

3. *Giriko*. The powder (*ko*) is a rosin mixture for gloves, which helps prevent them from becoming slippery. This is kept in small flasks with a screw-on cap or stick-in closure. These small flasks function at the same time as a handle (*netsuke*) for the string rolls.

4. *Fudeko* (*fude* = hairpin; *ko* = powder), also called *yunde* (bow hand) powder, is a gray powder for the bow hand; it contains potassium and is made by incinerating hide. This has a degreasing effect and thus also cleans the grip and restores a good hold. For storing this, salt shakers with cap covers have proven useful. To apply fudeko, the archer puts a bit of it on the left hand and rubs the hand and the grip of the bow together. In this way the hand is dried and the grip of the bow is cleaned at the same time. Any leftover powder is blown off.

5. *Magasune*, which literally means "medicine rubber," obviously a nickname from ancient times, is a little cloth woven out of old bowstrings. It is used before and after shooting to rub natural bowstrings until they are warm in order to redistribute the resin on them.

6. *Doho*, literally "road treasure," is a device for making string wrappings. The origin of its name is not entirely clear; it might be either a nickname or a proper name, possibly that of its inventor. The doho is composed of two flat pieces of wood between which the nakashikake (nocking-point reinforcement) can be pressed and rounded.

7. *Tobera* is a slender spatula used for all gluing operations. The end is slightly bent and tapers to a point.

8. *Bondo*, is glue. For most gluing operations, one only needs a simple white carpenter's glue. However, if one is using arrows

with aluminum shafts, it is a good idea to carry a contact cement.

9. *Boiled bowstrings.* For making wrappings for bowstrings, old bowstrings that have been boiled serve quite well. Also very good for making wrappings is hemp of the sort plumbers use.

10. *Replacement nocks and points.* The archer should carry an assortment of replacement nocks and points corresponding to the diameter of his arrows.

11. *Sandpaper.* The archer needs sandpaper of not too coarse a grain to clean the leather of the bow grip and to remove vestiges of glue. Since shooting for a long time can also easily produce calluses on the left hand, which often cause pain from pressure or abrasion, many archers carefully use sandpaper to rub their calluses off.

12. *Scissors or knife.*

13. *Twine or silk thread* is necessary for holding feathers fast while gluing as well as for underwrappings in the case of arrowheads that are too large or nocks that are too small, and for wrapping arrow shafts at the nock and feathers.

14. *Nigirigawa* (grip leather). If the leather of the bow grip becomes too dirty or damaged, it has to be changed. For a grip, one needs about three and a half turns around the bow for wide leather and about five and a half for narrow leather. Looking at the bow when held in the normal way, the leather is wrapped from the left on top toward the right on the bottom. The sharp-trimmed ends are inserted underneath and fastened with a little glue. To suit the size and shape of the archer's hand, one creates an underlayer of thick paper between the bow and the grip leather to assure an optimal shape for gripping.

10

BASIC TECHNIQUE OF THE HEKI SCHOOL

Tʜɪꜱ ᴄʜᴀᴘᴛᴇʀ ɪꜱ concerned with the setup of the shot according to the system of the Heki Ryu. The individual stages (*hassetsu*) will be described and a detailed commentary given. The serious practitioner is referred in this connection to chapter 13, "Correcting Common Mistakes," which contains further instructions and connects them with the basic technique.

PREPARATORY MOVEMENTS

The archer stands at the base line (*honza*) and holds the bow with the left hand and the arrows with the right at his sides at the level of his hips (fig. 10.1). The upper tip of the bow at this point is about 10 centimeters above the floor. The arrows are held by the heads and point backward in symmetry with the bowstring. The archer performs a standing bow (*tachirei*) in the direction of the target and steps forward—beginning with the left foot—in three steps to the shooting position (*shai*). There he turns the left foot

FIGURE 10.1

FIGURE 10.2

FIGURE 10.3

at a right angle toward the right foot (fig. 10.2), then turns his entire body until he has the target to his left.

The archer places the bow tip on the floor in front of him, lets the string fall from the outside downward (fig. 10.3), and raises the bow so that he has the string in front of the middle of his body (fig. 10.4). The right hand now places the arrow against the bow from the front, the index finger of the bow hand holds the arrow, and the right hand pushes the arrow in two movements far enough forward so that the string can be put into the nock (figs. 10.5–10.6). The right hand now takes hold of the string about 25 centimeters below the nocked arrow and raises the bow with the arrow, so that the arrow comes to the level of the face (fig. 10.7). In this position, the archer carries out *ashibumi* (takes the stance).

FIGURE 10.4   FIGURE 10.5

FIGURE 10.6   FIGURE 10.7

ASHIBUMI (STANCE)

Ashibumi fixes the relationship between the archer's body and the target. Through a correct ashibumi, the body should be able to maintain a stable position at the moment of releasing the shot. The middle axis of the target disk makes a straight line with the tips of both feet of the spread legs. The distance between the feet corresponds to half the body height, or the draw length of the arrow. The feet are turned slightly outward and include an angle of from 60 to 90 degrees.

Execution: The archer looks at the target (fig. 10. 8) and makes a line with his gaze from the target across the ground to himself; he then sets his left foot on this imagined line (fig. 10.9). Then he looks again and finishes by putting his right foot also on the

FIGURE 10.8   FIGURE 10.9

imagined line (fig. 10.10). The following points should be especially heeded in executing this movement:

- The line between the toes of the two feet should run toward the target.
- The distance between the feet should be neither bigger nor smaller than half the archer's height.
- The angle between the two feet should be roughly 60 to 90 degrees (fig. 10. 11).

The bow with the arrow is then placed with the lower bow tip on the left kneecap. The left arm is naturally extended slightly sideward; the right hand is placed on the knot of the hakama ties,

FIGURE 10.10

FIGURE 10.12

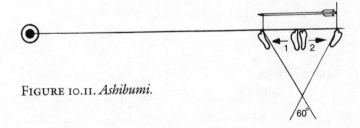

FIGURE 10.11. *Ashibumi.*

approximately at the navel, and rests there briefly. Then comes the *dozukuri* the balancing of the torso (fig. 10.12).

DOZUKURI (BALANCE)

Based on ashibumi, the body is now in a correct position, naturally erect yet stably set. Dozukuri should be done firmly yet without tensing up. Here the pelvis becomes the center of gravity as well as the link between the legs and the upper body. In order to make this connection stable, the pelvis is tilted slightly forward at the lower

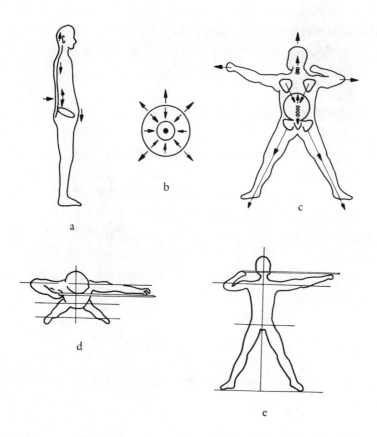

FIGURE 10.13. *Dozukuri (balance of the torso): (a, c) Vectors of force. (b) State of forces within the body. (d, e) Parallel lines in the position of the body.*

end, and the small of the back is slightly rounded. There should be a sensation of being locked in, in the area of the lower spine. The head is held erect and straight, the chin somewhat drawn in, and the gaze lowered to the ground about 2 to 3 meters in front of oneself. In this position, the archer should breathe in and out calmly once or twice; with the help of his right hand resting on his belly, he can feel and keep a check on the transference of movement from his diaphragmatic breathing. If dozukuri has been carried out correctly, the pelvis and both shoulders should be parallel to the line of ashibumi. The balance of the trunk thus achieved must be maintained throughout the entire shot (fig. 10.13a–e).

The form for dozukuri described here is for normal shooting at the 28-meter target or at the makiwara. Other forms of shooting require other forms of dozukuri. The following forms are distinguished:

- *Chunodozukuri:* central dozukuri, which is used for ordinary shooting.
- *Sorudozukuri:* backward-leaning dozukuri, used for long-distance shooting of 100 to 200 meters.
- *Kagarudozukuri:* forward-leaning dozukuri, used for shooting on horseback or while riding in boats.
- *Kakarudozukuri:* dozukuri leaning toward the left side, for low targets.
- *Nokudozukuri:* dozukuri leaning toward the right side, for high targets.

YUGAMAE (READYING THE BOW)

The preparations for shooting in yugamae include three movements:

1. *Torikake:* The right hand moves around the string and takes hold of the arrow.

2. *Tenouchi:* The bow hand takes a proper hold on the bow.
3. *Monomi:* The gaze goes to the target.

Torikake

The bow, while continuing to rest on the left knee, is moved back to the center of the body, so that the string is in front of the center of the body. At the same time, the right hand moves forward and is laid against the string about 15 centimeters below the arrow in such a way that the glove can be notched onto the string (figs. 10. 14 and 10.15). Next, first the top joint of the middle finger and then the top joint of the index finger are placed over the thumb — both exerting the same amount of pressure. The thumb should be notched onto the bowstring in such a way that the axis line runs lengthwise down the thumb and the string form a 90-degree angle. Without changing the position of the thumb, the middle finger, or the index finger, the hand is now slowly raised until the arrow lies on the index finger about 10 centimeters above the thumb. Through an inward twisting movement of the whole hand, the index finger presses the arrow both against the string and against the finger itself. One should not allow this movement to throw off the parallel relationship of the thumb axis and the arrow; indeed, this has to be maintained until hanare, the release of the shot (figs. 10.16 and 10.17).

Tenouchi

In Japanese archery, the bow hand has not only a static function to perform, but also has to press and turn actively in order to compensate for the asymmetry of the bow. This requires a special grip, which is known as *tenouchi*.

Execution: After torikake has been completed, bow and arrow are moved somewhat to the left, so that the right hand is positioned approximately in front of the left breast. The left hand is

FIGURE 10.14

FIGURE 10.15

FIGURE 10.16

FIGURE 10.17

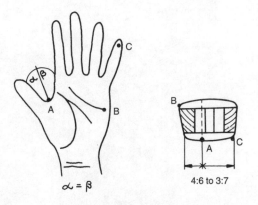

FIGURE 10.18. *Placement of the bow hand (tenouchi) on the bow. The points on the hand marked with letters are placed so as to cover the same letters on the bow.*

opened, so that a V is formed between the thumb and index finger. The bisector of this V angle is now laid on the bow in such a way that, looked at from the point of view of a cross-section of the bow, four parts lie to the left of this point of contact and six to the right (fig. 10.18). In forming the grip in this way, the skin between the thumb and the index finger is pressed onto the bow from below. This skin must remain pressed to the bow during the entire shot, since the transference of force that has to be accomplished by pushing and turning cannot be achieved if this point of contact (*tsunomi*) is lost (figs. 10.19 and 10.20). Then the line of the hand (*temonkin*) is placed on the back left edge of the bow, and the little finger curls around the bow. The little finger should come up as close to the level of the thumb as possible, but at the same time should only be placed as far back as the forward right edge of the bow; thus a distance will still remain to the back side of the bow that is big enough to pass a pencil through. In this way the smallest possible ring is formed between the thumb and the little finger. Into this space the ring finger and then the middle finger are tightly thrust. The nails of the three fingers form a straight line (fig. 10.21). The right hand does not change its position, but

FIGURE 10.19

FIGURE 10.20

the left hand presses the bow a little bit in the direction of the target, so that some tension is created (figs. 10.21 and 10.22).

Monomi

The gaze goes to the target. The head posture arrived at in this way is called *monomi*. In turning, the head should not be lowered but must remain vertical. The turning should also be performed naturally and without tensing up, and the other parts of the upper body should not move. Since the arrow is laid against the right

FIGURE 10.21

FIGURE 10.22. *In order to perform the function of the tsunomi, the hand must be placed in such a way that it is balanced in both planes.*

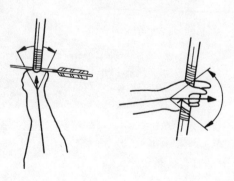

FIGURE 10.23

cheek for the remainder of the shot, it is important that the monomi always be carried out in the same way, since in altering this position the archer also changes the position of the right hand, and therefore will encounter difficulty when it comes to target shooting (fig. 10.23).

UCHIOKOSHI (RAISING THE BOW)

The purpose of uchiokoshi is to raise the bow—which at the end of yugamae is positioned diagonally to the left side—in such a way that the most comfortable position for starting to draw the bow is reached.

Execution: The right hand leads off the movement, raising the bow to the highest possible position. The shoulders remain unmoved during raising. During and after raising, the arrow should point somewhat downward. During raising, the hands do

FIGURE 10.24

not alter their position in the sideward directions; that is, the bow is neither drawn nor moved in the direction of the target (fig. 10.24).

SANBUN NO NI
(SECOND STEP TOWARD DRAWING THE BOW)

Sanbun no ni literally means, "the second of three." This means that sanbun no ni follows the first step (uchiokoshi) toward drawing the bow and precedes the last step, kai.

This position is also called *hikiwake* and means pulling equally to the right and left. This characterizes both the path from uchiokoshi to sanbun no ni and the end state of sanbun no ni itself.

Sanbun no ni has the following purposes:

- Preparing for *tsumeai*, the next stage

FIGURE 10.25

- Checking for the correct line of draw (direction of movement) of the right hand and of the right elbow
- Checking for correct and relaxed form in the shoulders
- Estimating the distance and position of the target

Execution: The left hand leads off the movement of drawing the bow. At the same time, the right hand joins in the movement and draws the arrow back to the level of the ear. The arrow is then also at the level of the eyebrows. The right hand is positioned over the right ear. Since the movement is initiated to the left, the tip of the arrow is still pointing slightly downward. This slight sloping downward of the arrow in the direction of the target is called *mizunagare*. This means that a drop of water can run off the arrow. During the drawing of the bow, the dozukuri should not be altered. In order to keep the right balance during the draw, the archer should imagine that with two-thirds force his left hand is pushing against the bowstring, and with one-third force his right arm is drawing the bow.

When he has reached the point of sanbun no ni, both hands stop their movement. The necessary application of force, however, does not stop (fig. 10.25).

TSUMEAI (REACHING MAXIMUM DRAW)

Tsumeai means driving a wedge into each arm joint and locking them off against each other. This ends the preparations for shooting.

Execution: The drawing motion of the left hand and the right elbow is continued, and the arrow is drawn to its full length. The length of the draw corresponds to half the height of the archer. Through the continuing movement of the right hand, the arrow finally touches the cheek of the archer just under the cheekbone. The touch of the arrow on the cheek is called *hozuke*. The bowstring touches the chest (*munazuru*). The left hand moves the bow so that the arrow is now horizontal and the archer can correctly aim at the target. In the state of tsumeai, the ashibumi line, the pelvis, the shoulders, and the arrow are all parallel (figs. 10.30 and 10.13).

NOBIAI (STRETCHING, EXTENDING)

In *nobiai*, the arrow keeps the position of tsumeai, but the entire force of the body is further increased and maximized toward the final extension. To do this, both shoulders must be stretched outward to the uttermost point, and force must be put into the legs. The position of the pelvis must be stabilized, and the spine must be stretched vertically upward, as though one were going to stick one's head through the ceiling.

The bow hand begins, with increasing strength, to push and turn, turning the right edge of the bow in the direction of the tar-

FIGURE 10.26

get. The right arm continues to pull further, and—from a certain point that must be thought of as a fist's breadth inward from the elbow—turns slightly inward (*hineru*) in such a way that the continuation of this movement will make it possible, when the bow hand makes its last push, for the bowstring to spring out of the notch in the glove (fig. 10.26).

YAGORO (CONTINUATION OF NOBIAI)

The stretching of nobiai is continued until the maximum point is reached. The body must remain solidly in place at this point so that the arrow can no longer be pulled out of its line of aim. The pushing and turning of the bow hand and the pulling of the right hand are continued until the release occurs.

HANARE (RELEASE)

From a physical point of view, hanare is the release of the bowstring from the thumb notch of the glove. At the same moment as this, the bow hand must continue its push with greater intensity in order to avoid misdirecting the arrow through a recoiling of the edge of the bow away from the target. This last push must become a conditioned reflex through long practice, so that the hanare can be actualized without thought. The state of the archer during hanare has been rendered in the following Japanese poem:

> YA O KAKETE
> HIKISHIBORURU WA
> OBOYU RO ZO
> HANARE DOKI NI WA
> MUNEN MUSO NI

> *When shooting an arrow*
> *As you fully extend the draw*
> *You might awaken.*
> *At the moment of release*
> *There is no thought, no idea.*

ZANSHIN (REFLECTION)

Zanshin can be understood in two ways. If *shin* is written as *mi*, it means "body." Zanshin is then understood as the form of the body that remains behind. The use and the direction of the forces that are put into play during tsumeai and nobiai determine this form that remains behind. If, however, *shin* is written as *kokoro* (literally, "heart"), it means "mind" or "soul." *Zanshin* is then translated as the return of ideas and thoughts after the highest point of concentration. This return of thoughts requires some time. During this time the gaze remains directed toward the flying arrow and then the place where it has struck.

This means that, although there is an ideal form of zanshin made up of both of the components mentioned above, the archer should not intentionally produce them, for then zanshin is no longer the result of the mental and physical forces previously at

FIGURE 10.27

work. The archer should be capable of understanding and interpreting his zanshin (figs. 10.27 and 10.30 a and b). For a delineation of the distinction between the right and wrong form of zanshin, please see chapter 13, "Correcting Common Mistakes."

Of course, the above should not be taken to mean that zanshin is an arbitrary result. The archer must have a conception of the correct zanshin; this must stand before him as a goal. It is often said when a sloppy zanshin occurs, "Let zanshin be the starting point of your thinking" ("*Zanshin kara kagaete*").

YUDAOSHI (LOWERING THE BOW)

After zanshin is over, the bow and the right hand are brought back calmly to the hips. Next the head is turned back and again faces straight forward. First the right and then the left foot are returned to their starting position. The archer then turns his body

FIGURE 10.28

90 degrees to the left, gazes at the target, and performs a standing bow to the target, before, with three backward steps (starting with the right foot), he returns to the honza (fig. 10.28).

ABOUT HANARE (RELEASE)

All the efforts of the archer to set up his shot correctly and properly end in hanare, and hanare is without a doubt one of the most difficult aspects of kyudo. The proper, timely, and dynamic coordination of all movements leading up to hanare can hardly be described in words, but can only be experienced in their complexity through the example of an advanced archer. For kyudoka who may have to practice by themselves, the lack of a model for hanare is frequently a major obstacle. It is true that one can get some help from film clips, but these help the archer little in learning the movements themselves. The hands and shoulders have to turn what they have seen in a film with their eyes or heard described in words into a reality, and often a long time passes before the hand is able to perform a movement consistently, and the archer may develop the impression that his practice is futile or wrong. Therefore, it seems to make sense for the archer to come to an understanding of the purpose of the individual movements and on that basis to attempt to develop the right feeling for the movement of hanare.

The goal of archery is to hit the target in a correct manner, that is, to shoot with good, balanced basic form without missing the target. In accordance with the strength of one's bow, one should shoot the fastest and most penetrating arrow possible. Physically this means that the center of gravity of the arrow in flight must be approximately in the middle of the shaft, and no extraneous movements must be allowed to hinder the arrow's flight. In order to be able to shoot in a fast and penetrating way, a sharp and precise hanare is necessary.

To begin with, let us consider the work of the left hand. Since the Japanese bow is built asymmetrically, and since there is no accommodation for the arrow, the archer has to handle the bow during shooting in such a way that, in spite of this, the arrow flies straight, for the asymmetry of the bow has the result that the lower limb of the bow moves forward faster after the release than the longer upper limb. Since the string runs up the center of the bow, at the moment of release the direction of the arrow would be diverted considerably to the right if at the last moment one did not turn the edge of the bow to the side. For this reason, at the release the left hand has to speed up the action of the slower upper limb of the bow by exerting downward pressure on the bow, and the little finger has to "catch" the faster lower limb. In order to compensate for the sideward deviation, the bow hand has to turn the edge of the bow to the left (fig. 10.31). To bring these required forces to bear on the bow, a special grip is needed, tenouchi. Tenouchi is considered the simplest and most comfortable way to hold the bow in order to carry out

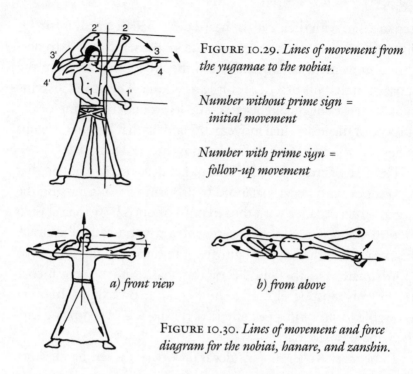

FIGURE 10.29. *Lines of movement from the yugamae to the nobiai.*

Number without prime sign = initial movement

Number with prime sign = follow-up movement

a) front view *b) from above*

FIGURE 10.30. *Lines of movement and force diagram for the nobiai, hanare, and zanshin.*

these two movements—pushing and turning. The ideal form of tenouchi is also called *momijigasane*. There are two interpretations of this concept.

1. *Momiji* = baby's hand. This means that the archer's grip should be firm but unstrained, like a child's (palmar reflex).
2. *Momiji* = maple. In the spring, the maple is pale green, and in the fall it becomes red—just as the fingernails do as a result of the pressure of grasping the bow.

The momiji has two functions: *uaoshi* ("push upward") and *nejiru* ("to turn" like a screw).

The contact position of the left hand on the bow in the 3 to 7 or 4 to 6 relationship (figs. 10.18 and 10.22) is called tsunomi. However, a correct grip and the proper contact position referred

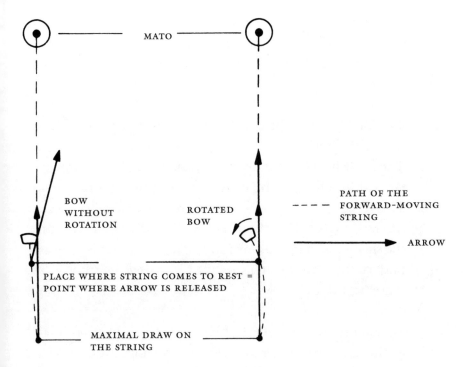

MATO

BOW
WITHOUT
ROTATION

ROTATED
BOW

PATH OF THE
FORWARD-MOVING
STRING

ARROW

PLACE WHERE STRING COMES TO REST =
POINT WHERE ARROW IS RELEASED

MAXIMAL DRAW ON
THE STRING

FIGURE 10.31

to as tsunomi—that is, the outer forms alone—are worthless by themselves. The two functions uaoshi and nejiru, together with that outer form, constitute the proper use of the left hand. This is *tsunomi no hataraki*, the "work of the tsunomi." Only tsunomi no hataraki as a whole produces the right action at the moment of hanare (fig. 10.30 a and b).

The distribution of the entire force exercised by the left hand is described as a 7- to 3- relationship of turning to pushing.

The priority placed on turning becomes comprehensible when one considers that the bow can only really be turned on its lengthwise axis once the string has been released from the thumb notch. Approximately in the first half of the short time the string takes to speed from full draw to a state of rest, the edge of the bow has to be turned aside in order to prevent the arrow from being diverted to the right.

In comparison with the left hand, the right can be quickly and successfully trained, once torikake can be correctly executed. The work of the right arm and the right hand then consists essentially in three movements (fig. 10.30 a and b):

1. The focal point of the drawing power continues to reside in the right elbow.
2. The angle between the upper arm and forearm is slightly increased, and this tensing delivers the remaining force.
3. The forearm and hand continue to turn steadily inward (*hineri*), so that the bowstring can gradually free itself from the string notch in the glove and be torn out of it by the last push of the left hand. This is called *hinerikoto*, which has the sense "fast turn."

According to *Kyudo Nyumon*, "Hineri has the function of allowing the force of the draw to keep growing stronger in a steady continuous way up to hanare. Hineri makes hanare strong and creates a basis for hitting the target. In order to bring the hineri of the right hand to completion, the yunde also performs a hineri with a corresponding amount of force that pushes the bow downward. The hineri direction of the right hand brings the wrist into one direction with the arrow; the hineri turning of the yunde keeps the grip on the bow through tenouchi in one direction."

When the turning of the right hand comes not from the elbow but instead from the wrist, the wrist buckles and the shot cannot free itself from the thumb groove. When optimal coordination occurs, all the movements of the left and right hands come together in the moment that brings about the release. The simultaneous working together of the hinerikoto and the tsunomi no hataraki produces the essence of the Heki Insai Ha (Insai branch of the Heki Ryu), namely, *kan* and *chu* (speed and power of penetration).

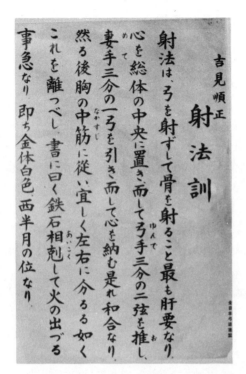

FIGURE 10.32

A remark by the ancient Japanese master archer Yoshimi Daigemon on the principle of proper archery has been handed down: "One should shoot not only with the bow but also with the mind and technique of a traditional, orthodox school. To this end one should gather the mind at the center of the body. The left hand pushes the string with two-thirds [of the maximum possible force]; the right hand draws the bow with one-third [of the total force]. Then, by holding the mind properly at the center of the body, the right balance in shooting will be produced. The release should happen from the middle of the chest in equal parts to the left and right. A master said: 'The release must be like a spark that arises from iron and stone striking together!' When an archer has absorbed this teaching, he will understand the appearance of the morning star at twilight and of the new moon in the west." (The text of this commentary is shown in fig. 10.32.)

BREATHING PATTERNS AND RHYTHM OF MOVEMENTS

The approximate sequence of movements and the customary pattern of breathing that goes with them are described in figure 10.33. The rhythm indicated here, however, is only a recommendation. Especially for beginners, it is difficult to get from the uchiokoshi to the zanshin in only one breath. If this is the case, it is a good idea to begin with an in-breath when raising the bow, to breathe out until the sanbun no ni, to breathe in again there, then to breathe out again during the transition to the tsumeai, to suspend the breath during the tsumeai, nobiai, and the yagoro, and then breathe out during the zanshin and the yudaoshi. But if the archer does not find this pattern possible, he should breathe in and out as he has to. However, in that case, he should make sure that breathing and movement are coordinated with each other. The general rule is that during strenuous movements, such as drawing, one should breathe out. All during shooting one should breathe only from the diaphragm. That is, with the in-breath the abdomen swells out slightly, because the diaphragm comes down; and during the out-breath, the abdomen again flattens out somewhat. This has the result that during the flexing of the abdominal muscles, the trunk is drawn yet more firmly into the pelvis, and thus the position of dozukuri is consolidated by the out-breath at stages of active exertion.

STANDING AND SITTING

In standing and sitting (fig. 10.34), the kyudoka should always maintain a natural, upright position. The same goes for the transition from standing to sitting and vice versa. The spine, within the range of its natural back-and-forth movement, remains vertical; whether at rest or in movement, neither head nor seat should

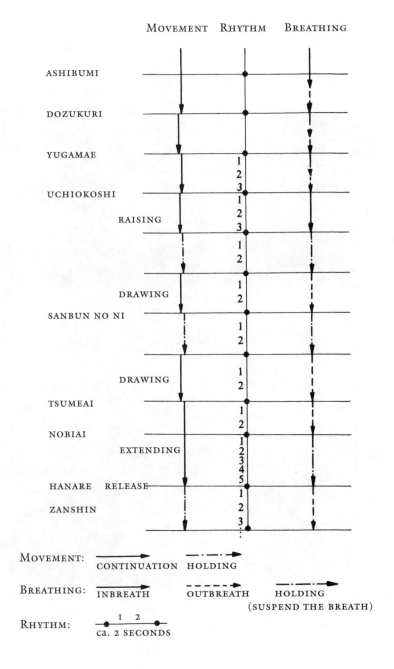

MOVEMENT   RHYTHM   BREATHING

ASHIBUMI

DOZUKURI

YUGAMAE
                                    1
                                    2
                                    3
UCHIOKOSHI   1
                                    2
            RAISING   3

                                    1
                                    2

            DRAWING   1
                                    2
SANBUN NO NI

                                    1
                                    2

            DRAWING   1
                                    2
TSUMEAI   1
                                    2
NOBIAI   1
            EXTENDING   2
                                    3
                                    4
                                    5
HANARE   RELEASE   1
ZANSHIN   2
                                    3

MOVEMENT: ———————▶   — · — · ▶
           CONTINUATION   HOLDING

BREATHING: ========▶   — — — — ▶   — · — · — ▶
            INBREATH   OUTBREATH   HOLDING
                                         (SUSPEND THE BREATH)

RHYTHM: •——1——2——•
            ca. 2 SECONDS

FIGURE 10.33. *Breath and Movement Rhythm.*

FIGURE 10.34. *Standing and sitting.*

protrude in such a way as to depart from its natural center of gravity.

Nose and navel are in a vertical line, the back of the head is slightly stretched upward, the ears are over the shoulders.

The feet are parallel and about 4 centimeters apart. In sitting, the two big toes touch, with the back of the feet resting extended on the floor.

The weight of the body is always balanced equally on both legs.

The gaze rests on the ground about 4 meters in front of the archer while standing and about 2 meters in front while sitting, without the head being sunk forward.

11

AIMING AND
TARGET SHOOTING

Since in kyudo, direct aiming—as in rifle shooting—is impossible, the student must understand the special characteristics of aiming in kyudo.

After assimilating the basics on a theoretical level, the student must begin by shooting at the target from a reduced distance and then, finally, as confidence increases, become able to shoot at the target from the standard distance of 28 meters. In order to be able to hit the target with certainty, in addition to initial observations from his trainer, the archer must give special attention to the following points, which always need to be carried out:

1. Correctly nocking the arrow on the bowstring. For this, the lower part of the shaft is laid against the leather of the grip. To begin with, the nock is at an angle of 90 degrees to the string, and that is shifted upward by approximately the width of one nock (fig. 11.1).
2. Torikake must be precise from its first application to the

moment of hanare; that is, the lengthwise axis of the thumb always remains parallel to the arrow (fig. 10.17).

3. The contact position of the bow hand must assure an even resting place for the arrow. The lower edge of the arrow should continue to lie against the upper edge of the leather of the grip once the hand has taken its position. This means the tsunomi must be executed in such a way that the arrow can maintain a constant position (figs. 11.2 and 10.21).

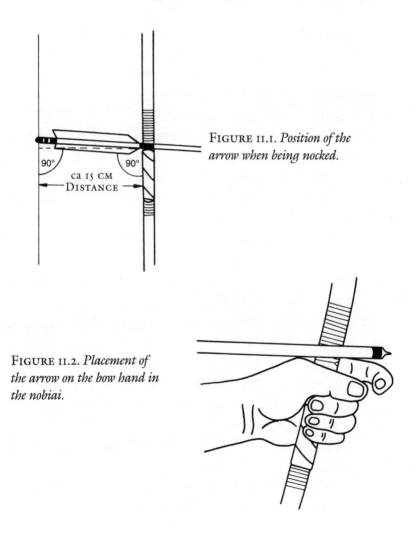

FIGURE 11.1. *Position of the arrow when being nocked.*

FIGURE 11.2. *Placement of the arrow on the bow hand in the nobiai.*

4. Contact of the arrow against the cheek: hozuke (fig. 10.26).
5. The relationship of the target to the bow must be seen properly by the archer after having been given the needed corrections (fig. 11.3 and 11.4).
6. The arrow absolutely must be horizontal during nobiai and hanare.

PRACTICAL EXERCISES

To begin with, the trainer shoots four mato arrows at the earthen embankment of the target area from a distance of about 7 meters with the student's bow and arrows. At the level determined in this way by the arrows that stick, a target is hung, at which the student is to shoot from the same distance.

Once the student has fully drawn the bow (nobiai, hozuke, the arrow horizontal), the trainer sights over the arrow and corrects the position of the student's left hand until the imagined extension of the arrow points directly into the middle of the target. The student should notice how he sees the target in relation to the bow, and then when he is ready, he should shoot the arrow (fig. 11. 3).

Since the direction of the arrow cannot be visually corrected by the student himself, help here at the beginning is indispensable. The archer has the following opportunities to be sure of getting the sideways direction right.

1. Ashibumi and dozukuri must be carried out correctly, since they already determine the position of the body in relation to the target.
2. The position of the right hand must be felt through the hozuke.
3. The position of the left hand can be controlled by the eye. At full draw, the right eye looks at the bow, and the left eye looks past the bow at the target. A mixed picture comes

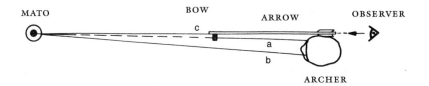

FIGURE II. 3. *a) View of the right eye. b) View of the left eye. c) Line of aim.*

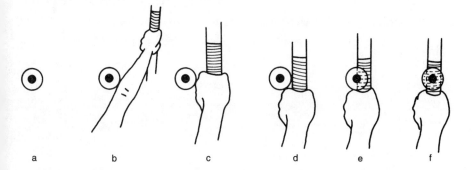

FIGURE II.4. *Ways of seeing the target.*
a) yugamae (monomi)
b) uchiokoshi (approx. next to the left elbow)
c) sambun no ni (approx. next to the back of the left hand)
d–e) tsumeai and nobiai
Depending on the nature of the bow, the target appears as (d) rising moon
(ariake) or (e) half moon.
f) full moon

about from this way of sighting, in which, depending on the nature of the bow, at the time of correction the target appears to be more or less on top of or to the side of the bow (fig. II.4).

If the mato is missed in spite of the side-view correction, the fault that led to the misdirection of the arrow has to be recognized. Under no circumstances should misses due to wrong direction or wrong height be compensated for by wrong aiming. Proper aiming and striking the target are the object of the exercise. Striking the target as a result of combining faults in shooting is worthless.

If the student hits the target from a short distance, the distance to the target can be increased step by step. Recommended stages are 7 meters, 14 meters, 20 meters, and 28 meters. The height of the target, which is different for every distance, should be determined as described above.

In addition, adjustment of the sideward position and the visual registration of the target require continual supervision from trainers or fellow archers during the beginning period.

12

TEACHING BEGINNERS

I F   A   V I S I T O R   to a dojo who is interested in kyudo seriously expresses the intention of beginning with kyudo himself in the near future, it is a good idea for an advanced student or a trainer to have a chat with the interested party to clarify matters. Since kyudo is still not widely known, and since there are frequently misunderstandings about the practice and its goal, it has proven useful to question the would-be beginner in this conversation about his reasons for wishing to begin to study kyudo, what he hopes to get out of it, and whether he is well informed about the practice and its methods. It should be especially pointed out to the beginner that the practice of Japanese archery requires a great deal of time and patience, and that anyone who wants to make progress in it will have to practice regularly. The fact that it will be some time before the student can take his first shot at the target should certainly not be passed over. If, on the basis of his own statements and the impression he makes on the trainer, a beginner still seems ready to practice kyudo, then he should be taken on as a student.

In the first hour of practice, one should give the beginning student an explanation of shooting and the special characteristics of the shooting technique. He should get a rough understanding of the significance of the individual stages and the relationship between them. This preliminary knowledge should then be deepened through reading chapter 10, "Basic Technique of the Heki School," and by repeated observation of other archers while the beginner is shooting at the makiwara and the mato. Before receiving practical instruction, the beginner should be told the rules of dojo etiquette and rei.

It is especially important to point out that the bow and arrow are real weapons and must be handled carefully, with a view to safety.

The first practical exercises are carried out exclusively with an apparatus roughly resembling a slingshot. The apparatus (*gomuyumi*, "rubber bow") consists of a wrapped grip that corresponds to the shape of the bow grip, with two attached rounded lengths of natural rubber that are connected to each other. With this simple apparatus, all the stages of shooting can be effectively simulated.

Here are some general points to heed when practicing with the rubber practice bow:

- The rubber practice bow should be adjusted in length and pull strength to suit the student. Depending on the case, it should be shortened or lengthened; or only the inner or outer piece of rubber may be used in the drawing exercises.
- When drawing it, one always holds the rubber practice bow in such a way that the loop makes a half turn around the grip on the side away from the archer. In this way the force needed to turn the bow is simulated, and at the time of hanare, the rubber cannot strike the hand or the face.
- The grip is attached to the rubber loop in such a way that the contact position of the left hand is about 2 centimeters below the opening in the rubber.

HOW TO USE THE RUBBER PRACTICE BOW

One should explain to the new beginner once again the significance of the bow hand and the function that tenouchi has to fulfill. In connection with this, the first thing to practice with the rubber practice bow is correct placement of the tenouchi on the grip. Once the grip has been correctly executed, the preparations for shooting can begin. These preparations include work on rei, the sequence of steps, the posture of the arms and hands, and behavior after the shot. Only after the completion of this preparatory phase should step-by-step training in the individual stages of the hassetsu begin. A good training sequence would be as follows:

- The student stands in front of the makiwara, the mato, or a suitable substitute.
- The grip on the rubber practice bow is executed correctly (figs. 12.1 and 12.2). The rubber practice bow, held with a proper tenouchi, is then moved to the hip as with a bow. The right hand is accordingly also brought to the right hip.
- This is followed by tachirei to the target.
- Beginning with the left foot, the archer takes three steps toward the target and then turns the body 90 degrees.
- Execution of ashibumi; that is, the gaze goes to the target, the left foot is set, the gaze is done again, and the right foot is set. The distance between the feet is half a body length; the angle of the feet is about 60 degrees; and the line to the target runs across the tips of the toes (fig. 12.3).
- Dozukuri. The left hand holds the rubber practice bow in front of the body as it would the bow. The right hand is held in front of the abdomen. Care should be taken to correct the posture of the pelvis, torso, shoulders, and head; and these should be corrected if necessary. Special attention should be paid to breathing and gaze (fig. 12.4).

FIGURE 12.1

FIGURE 12.2

FIGURE 12.3

FIGURE 12.4

FIGURE 12.5

- Yugamae. A proper grip of the bow with the left hand has already been achieved. Thus tenouchi does not need to be carried out during yugamae. In a way corresponding to the way the grip is done with the glove on, during torikake phase, the loop of the rubber practice bow is slipped over the thumb, and the index and ring fingers are laid over the end of the thumb. The fingers and thumb should not be tensed into a cramped position, since otherwise release with the rubber practice bow is barely possible (fig. 12.5). In particular, if the thumb is formed into a hook, then at hanare, the rubber cannot readily slip away.

The following preliminary drawing of the rubber must be carried out by the left hand. During yugamae, one should be sure that the necessary movements come only from the arms, and that the shoulders are not moved along with them. Also, the balance of torso and head positions achieved during the dozukuri should not be lost. The gaze to the target (monomi) should be accompanied by an out-breath (fig. 12.6).

- Uchiokoshi. The right hand raises the rubber practice bow, and the left hand follows along. This is accompanied by an

FIGURE 12.6

FIGURE 12.7

FIGURE 12.8

FIGURE 12.9

in-breath. In consideration of the (absent) arrow, one should make sure that the rubber points a little downward to the left. A fault that is often observed in beginners is that, during raising, the grip of the rubber practice bow does not remain vertical but is held crooked with a stiff wrist. This requires the appropriate correction (fig. 12.7).

- Sanbun no ni. The left hand begins the drawing of the bow, and the right hand follows after. This is accompanied by an out-breath. The rubber is now over the eyebrows, and the right thumb is about a fist's breadth away from the ear (fig. 12.8).

- Kai: the full draw. At this point, the rubber, like the arrow, should be placed just below the cheekbone. The rubber is now horizontal. The posture of the shoulders, arms, and hands should be observed and corrected.

When a student is able to execute the individual positions correctly up to this point, he should begin — through pushing and turning with the left hand and inward turning of the right hand — to prepare for hanare (fig. 12.9).

FIGURE 12.10

- Hanare and zanshin should be understood and interpreted as the result of the forces that have been put in play leading up to them. Added movements after the fact are without value. In order to make the hanare easier for the archer, especially as concerns the work of the right hand, one can place an arrow through the opening between the thumb and index finger of the right hand. It is then easier for the beginner to execute the turn against the pseudo string, and thus to release the rubber correctly (fig. 12.10).

It is a good idea when the beginner is practicing with the rubber practice bow to proceed in a step-by-step fashion and to have him keep repeating all the steps from the beginning.

PHASES OF PRACTICE

1. We may regard the initial goal of practice as the beginner's ability to achieve and hold a correct grip on the rubber practice bow and master drawing it properly. Before doing hanare with the rubber practice bow, the beginner should pursue, as the second goal of practice, the proper sequential timing and coordination of breath and movement.

During this phase of practice it is indispensable for every shot by the beginner to be observed and corrected by an advanced archer.

2. When the shooting sequence with the rubber practice bow has been correctly learned, the student begins performing the hassetsu exclusively with the real bow; that is, he practices the draw as far as nobiai. Under no circumstances should the string of a fully drawn bow be released without an arrow. If one does this, there is a high degree of risk that the bow will break.

This phase of training is also the time to familiarize the student with the general handling of the bow, such as drawing and undrawing it, the care of the bow and bowstrings, and so on. During execution of the individual hassetsu movements, emphasis should be placed during this phase of training on application of tenouchi to the bow and maintenance of tenouchi during the draw. For this reason, along with working with the bow, practice shooting with the rubber practice bow should be continued.

3. Once the individual movements are correct, training with the bow, glove, and arrow at the makiwara begins. Correct execution and maintenance of the torikake are special goals of practice during this phase. Initially here too, the bow is only drawn as far as the nobiai and unbent again without shooting.

Once the form and the coordination of timing are correct, one tries to lead the student from nobiai to hanare. Hanare is forbidden so long as torikake is still not sure, since otherwise the arrow can easily fall from the hand and fly off uncontrolled.

Also in this phase of practice, it is desirable for the student to be constantly observed by an advanced archer. One way of bringing this about is for the beginner and the advanced archer to shoot at the makiwara together; in this way, mutual observation and learning from each other is possible.

If experienced kyudoka are unavailable, beginners necessarily have to correct one another. Corrections in that case should never contain an *opinion* about the observed shot and the faults involved in it, but only points that one has been able to observe *in actual fact*.

Regarding shooting faults, the relationships of the various factors involved are often very complicated, and matters can be made even worse through false corrections (see chapter 13, "Correcting Common Mistakes").

Important phases in learning kyudo—such as the first release or the first shot at a target—always require guidance from an advanced archer.

4. Once a kyudoka is already capable of releasing an arrow at the makiwara, he will then spend considerable time trying to improve his shooting at the makiwara. Experience suggests that

training up to the point of the first release requires about half a year. This corresponds in the degree system to the fifth kyu.

5. In the half-year that follows, during the stage of practice leading to the fourth kyu degree, the student should be able to execute the hassetsu sequence smoothly and correctly enough so that it is possible to begin with mato shooting at the end of the second half-year. During this stage of practice, the student should be shown how to handle all the equipment that is necessary for archery (see "Rules for Examinations" in chapter 15). During this period of time, the forms for examinations and competitions should be taught along with the actual shooting technique.

6. In the following stages of practice, shooting at the makiwara continues to be of major importance. Although the student should also shoot at the mato and should have understood the principle of aiming more or less from the third kyu on, at this stage shots still go off in an uncertain and widely scattered fashion, since presumably a number of shooting mistakes are still present. For the student at this level, shooting at the mato primarily has the purpose of acquainting him with the relationship between his shooting form and the shooting results he achieves, and of allowing him to work on the errors in question at the makiwara. It has proven useful for the student to shoot four arrows at the mato and then twelve at the makiwara, since shooting mistakes can be worked on significantly more effectively at the straw bale—uninfluenced by the bull's eye—than at the mato.

For candidates for the first kyu, however, it is best that at the beginning of a training session—more or less as a warm-up exercise—four shots should be shot at the makiwara and then the majority of shots at the mato.

For correction of mistakes, however, at all levels of practice, work at the makiwara is indispensable.

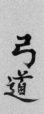

13

CORRECTING COMMON MISTAKES

A MAN WHO was learning archery once took his position before the target with two arrows. Thereupon his teacher corrected him: "Beginners should never shoot with two arrows at a time; otherwise they rely on the second one and deal carelessly with the first. They're better off leaving all calculations aside and having the conviction that the whole outcome depends on the one arrow they have already placed in the bow."*

Of course, we should scarcely presume that anyone who was with his teacher and had two arrows would behave heedlessly with them, but for the most part students are rarely aware of their negligence, while it never escapes the teacher.

COMMON MISTAKES

ASHIBUMI

1. The right foot is in front of or behind the shooting line.
2. The distance between the feet is too great or too small.

* From the *Tsurezuregusa* by Yoshida Kenko (1283–ca. 1350).

3. The angle of the feet is too great.
4. The angle of the feet is too small.

Dozukuri

5. The left side of the pelvis is too high.
6. The right side of the pelvis is too high.
7. The pelvis is twisted either to the right or the left out of the horizontal.
8. The back is rounded as a result of bad pelvis posture.
9. The body is leaning backward.
10. The upper body is leaning forward.
11. The upper body is tilted toward the target.
12. The upper body is tilted to the right.
13. The entire body is twisted to the right.

Yugamae

14. The left shoulder is too low.
15. The bow is held incorrectly.
16. The hand is too low in performing tenouchi.
17. The hand is too high in performing tenouchi.
18. The left wrist is bent too far toward the back of the hand.
19. The left wrist is bent too far toward the inside of the hand.
20. The thumb of the right hand is pointing down.
21. The thumb of the right hand is pointing up.
22. Wrong head posture in monomi.
23. Weak neck musculature.

Uchiokoshi

24. The arrow is pointing upward.
25. The bow is not perpendicular.
26. Uchiokoshi is too fast.
27. Uchiokoshi is too slow.

Hikiwake/Sanbun no ni

28. In drawing the bow, the right hand is pulling too hard.
29. Sanbun no ni is too small.

30. Sanbun no ni is too big.
31. Sanbun no ni is too high.
32. Sanbun no ni is too low.
33. The right hand pulls harder than the left.
34. In drawing, the left hand pushes too fast.
35. Lingering in sanbun no ni.
36. Uneven movement in the draw.
37. Mistakes in drawing the bow.
38. The left shoulder is too high.
39. The left shoulder is too far back.
40. The right shoulder is too high.
41. The right shoulder is too far forward.
42. Mistakes in the movement of the left elbow.
43. The force for drawing the bow is developed from the right wrist rather than the elbow.
44. Loss of proper torikake.
     a. The wrist is bent.
     b. The thumb is on the top.
     c. Loss of the inward turn.
45. Mistake in the balance of force between the hands.

TSUMEAI
46. The bow is drawn too far.
47. The bow is not drawn far enough.
48. The munazuru is missing.
49. The hozuke is too high.
50. The hozuke is too low.
51. Aiming error resulting from upset balance

NOBIAI
52. Disruption of the balance of forces in drawing the bow and in breathing during nobiai.
     a. *hayake* (premature release).
     b. *busuki* (shooting without enthusiasm).
     c. *chijimi* (relaxing tension of right arm).

53. Yurumi (right arm moves in direction of target).
54. Chijimi.
55. The upper body leans toward the target.
56. The upper body leans to the right.

HANARE

57. Imprecise tenouchi.
58. The wrist is bent inward.
59. The wrist is bent outward.
60. The wrist is tilted too far downward.
61. The wrist is bent too far upward.
62. The left shoulder is too high or is collapsing backward.
63. The left shoulder is too low.
64. The left shoulder is too far forward.
65. Wrong *yugaeri* (rotation of bow after hanare) resulting from throwing the wrist back.
66. Wrong yugaeri resulting from opening the bow hand.
67. Wrong midpoint for turning the bow.
68. At hanare the arms are moved upward.
69. The left hand and the upper body are thrust too far in the direction of the target.
70. Opening the right hand to bring about hanare.
71. Moving the right hand back at hanare.
72. Moving the right elbow back at hanare.
73. Incorrect inward turning of the right wrist or failure to execute the inward turning.
74. Use of a glove that does not fit.
75. Hayake (premature release) as a result of the bow being too strong.
76. Hayake resulting from inadequate concentration.
77. Hayake resulting from a weak tsunomi.
78. Hayake resulting from wrong breathing.
79. Unnecessary movement of the head at hanare.
80. Rearward lean of the body during hanare.

Shot Results of the Errors. This overview presumes that the faults appear singly; it does not take into account chains of faults.

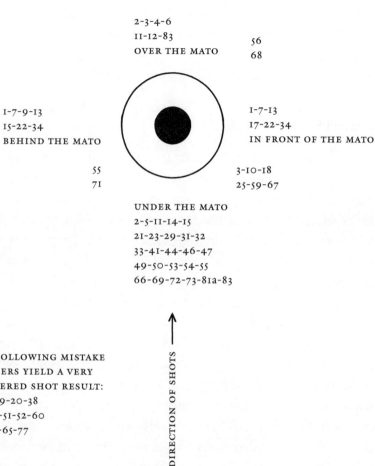

2-3-4-6
11-12-83
OVER THE MATO

56
68

1-7-9-13
15-22-34
BEHIND THE MATO

55
71

1-7-13
17-22-34
IN FRONT OF THE MATO

3-10-18
25-59-67

UNDER THE MATO
2-5-11-14-15
21-23-29-31-32
33-41-44-46-47
49-50-53-54-55
66-69-72-73-81a-83

THE FOLLOWING MISTAKE
NUMBERS YIELD A VERY
SCATTERED SHOT RESULT:
8-16-19-20-38
43-48-51-52-60
61-64-65-77

DIRECTION OF SHOTS →

81. Wrong arm posture during hanare.
82. Distortion of the face muscles.
83. Wrong moment for hanare.

ZANSHIN

84. Lack of mental tension at zanshin.
85. Loss of balance during hanare.
86. Too long or too short zanshin.

Errors in Concentration (87)

87a. Fear and inadequate confidence.

87b. Excessive concentration on hitting the mark.

87c. Excessive concentration during shooting.

87d. Arrogance and ambition.

87e. Concentration faults due to external circumstances.

PROBLEMS IN CORRECTION*

In kyudo there are two kinds of errors: (1) mistakes of a physical nature, and (2) lapses in concentration, in mindfulness in relation to oneself—in other words, errors of a mental kind. Both kinds of mistakes generally arise from not having practiced correctly, that is, having practiced without the necessary attentiveness. The best antidote to mistakes of all kinds is consistent and thorough practice of the basic technique. Returning to the basic technique when mistakes have been noticed leads with certainty to the desired success.

In practice this can mean having to go back and start from the beginning again—having to repeat once again stages of practice one thought one had left behind. Thus, for example, if the archer begins to experience fear about the release while using bow and arrow, it is a good idea to repeat this process again with the rubber practice bow. Also, when errors in drawing the bow occur, it is good to repeat this process a number of times with the rubber practice bow or else only with the bow, without arrow or glove, until the mistake has been eliminated.

"Being free of mistrust" (*kyoshin tankei*) is the spirit in which one should work on correcting one's mistakes.

This chapter and the list of common mistakes are intended to help us recognize errors and deal with them properly.

* Adapted from Genshiro Inagaki, *Kyudo Nyumon* (Tokyo: Shoten AF Publishing, 1971), chap. 5.

Often the unsuccessful shot results of different archers might be identical, but in each case one has to check through to be sure different causes are not at the source of these occurrences. For this reason, the analysis of mistakes is a very difficult but important aspect of kyudo training. That is why it is the supreme art of a trainer to correctly recognize shooting mistakes and to help set students on the right path toward solving their problems. Let us point out again that overly general, superficial correction as a rule has a counterproductive effect. A Japanese saying on this subject tells us the following: "If you correct the cow's horns too much, she will die" (*"Tsuno o tamete ushi o karosu"*).

If there is too much or inaccurate correction, and analysis is imprecise, it is quite possible that shooting mistakes will become worse or that new ones will appear. For this reason, we distinguish between individual mistakes and series or chains of mistakes.

Closely considering an archer, one will see that mistakes often have entirely different causes. In order really to be able to help him, the trainer must go back to the cause and see how a false movement continues to play out and influence the result. It is much simpler to correct an isolated fault.

In making corrections, we must also take into account whether the mistake is one that has just momentarily arisen, for example as a result of problems with external conditions, such as lengthy interruptions in practice or illness, or if the mistake is rooted in the archer's mental attitude.

The following example gives us an indication of how hard it is to work on a mistake in a truly effective manner. In 1932, Inagaki Sensei won the Tenranjiai (a competition that takes place in the presence of the emperor). During this competition he clearly noticed an unpleasant feeling in his right hand and concluded that this must be the result of a mistake, however slight. Then for years he tried to trace the source of this problem and even made use of technical aids like high-speed cameras to try to spot the cause. After about thirteen years, as he was telling his teacher about his efforts, the latter said to him, "Yes, you are right, it has gotten a little better." For this "little bit better" it took thirteen years. This shows how hard it is to combat a mistake with real effectiveness. In order to deal with shooting mistakes properly, no matter of what sort, a strong will is always necessary, for without it one easily becomes inattentive and falls back quickly into old patterns.

How do shooting mistakes arise in the first place? As a rule, the beginner is correctly instructed in the basic technique by an advanced archer or a teacher. And in fact, to begin with, the archer exhibits relatively few faults and willingly follows corrections. But if he practices for a period of time alone and shoots at the makiwara or mato on his own, it is during this phase that mistakes readily appear. The advanced archer, in addition to this, builds up his own opinion about his shooting over time and tries on his own to understand, interpret, or influence it. But since during the early years everything about correct shooting has yet to be understood and made into a corresponding reality, divergences from the basic technique are inevitable, and thus mistakes arise.

Another cause is human laziness. Since the inclination to take the seemingly easiest and most comfortable way out exists in kyudo as elsewhere, mistakes easily sneak in. One becomes unmindful of oneself and the technique one is executing in this state, and the result is evident in the shot results.

Proper practice thus requires a strong will and hard work on oneself. Let us stress again that faults can be avoided best through practicing the basic technique. One has to practice with a beginner's enthusiasm (*shoshin no kaere*). When you have had a mistake pointed out to you by another archer, you should make use of this incident, first to grasp the fault and its cause mentally, and then, during shooting, to pay precise attention to your physical form and the way the arrow flies.

In the following pages, the individual hassetsu (basic stages) are presented with their possible mistakes. Without a doubt, it would be possible to name still more mistakes in more detail.

The following enumeration is a representative selection of mistakes that appear frequently in the execution of the individual basic stages.

The mistakes are described independently as isolated faults. The possible relationship with prior mistakes—that is, the possible development of chains of mistakes—is not or hardly touched upon.

Since shooting mistakes also always influence the flight of the arrow and thus the shot results, with each mistake a typical picture of results at the target will be given. The descriptions are given from the point of view of the archer in yugamae. This means that when we say the arrow goes under the mato, it has been shot too short. If the description of the shot result says that the arrow goes over the mato, that means the shot has flown too high. The concept "The arrow goes in front of the mato" means that the arrow strikes to the right of the target. The concept "The arrow goes behind the mato" means that it strikes to the left of the target.

MISTAKES IN ASHIBUMI (1–4)

1. The right foot is in front of or behind the shooting line.

Shot result: If the right foot is in front of the shooting line, the arrows go behind the mato. If the right foot is behind the shooting line, the arrows go in front of the mato (fig. 13.1).

Correction: Proper execution of ashibumi with the proper directing of the gaze and, if necessary, supervision from a fellow archer.

2. The distance between the feet is too great or too small.

Shot result: If the distance between the feet is too great, the arrows go over the mato. If the feet are too close together, the arrow goes under the mato.

Correction: This is simply a matter of setting the feet at the right distance apart. This distance, as stated earlier, is half the

FIGURE 13.1

FIGURE 13.2

FIGURE 13.3

body height of the archer. However, if the archer has the habit of holding the shoulders very high during shooting, he is allowed to execute a somewhat wider ashibumi than prescribed. On the other hand, if an archer shoots with his shoulders very low, he should be allowed to do a somewhat narrower ashibumi (fig. 13.2).

3. The angle of the feet is too great (fig. 13.3).

If the angle included by the feet is too great, the following results are often produced:

- Balance becomes unsure, especially when the bow is fully drawn, and the upper body falls easily forward.
- Or the pelvis protrudes rearward. The lower back hollows out (swayback) beyond the acceptable point.
- The shoulders and the upper back become rounded, the face is too far forward, and the chin is pushed up.

Shot result: Arrows go in front of or under the mato. As a result of wrong sighting, the arrow can also go behind the mato.

Correction: The proper angle of between 60 and 90 degrees must be assumed. Heavier archers can choose a wider angle. Light, slender people can take a smaller angle, but never less than 60 degrees.

4. The angle of the feet is too small.

In the case of too small an angle, dozukuri will generally not be stable, and the upper body easily leans backward.

Shot result: The arrow goes behind the mato. This mistake, however, is also found when the dozukuri is not correct even though the feet have been set at the proper angle.

Correction: Assuming the proper angle (see correction for mistake #3). This correction is important for advanced kyudoka. A beginner often makes other mistakes that have a far greater effect on the flight of the arrow: for example, a bad dozukuri or holding the arms incorrectly. Only after these other mistakes are no longer being committed does it become essential to correct ashibumi.

MISTAKES IN DOZUKURI (5–13)

Bad Pelvic Posture

5. The left side of the pelvis is too high (fig. 13.4). With this the left shoulder is also too high.

Shot result: The shot is weak and as a rule goes under the mato.

Correction: The archer can himself feel whether the reinforced trapezoidal piece of the back of his hakama (hakama no kushita) is touching his back, thus reporting back to him the sensation of being straight. However, another archer can also watch to see if the hakama no kushita is touching the back in the correct fashion.

FIGURE 13.4   FIGURE 13.5

6. The right side of the pelvis is too high.

Since the right shoulder is also too high in this case, the shot is badly released by the right hand (fig. 13.5).

Shot result: Arrows go over the mato. One should pay attention in correcting this mistake to see if the archer might not be giving his right hand a quick extra rearward jerk at the moment of release, since arrows also go under the mato as a result of this movement.

Correction: As with mistake #5.

7. The pelvis is horizontal, but while remaining horizontal is twisted forward either on the left side or the right (fig. 13.6). With these pelvic positions, the shoulders are also correspondingly twisted out of place; which way they are twisted determines the path of the arrows—that is, too far in front of or too far behind the mato.

Correction: First of all, ashibumi has to be checked over, and then the position of the pelvis, to see if it is precise and straight;

FIGURE 13.6

FIGURE 13.7

then the shoulders have to be checked as to their position in relation to the pelvis. If, for some reason, it is not possible for a particular archer to have the lines through the feet, the pelvic bones, and the shoulders running parallel, then ashibumi can be altered so that the pelvis and the shoulders have the right relationship to the shooting line.

8. Bad pelvic posture resulting in a rounded back.

Because the pelvis has not been brought stably into place, the upper body is also unstable, with the result that arrows fly in a scattered fashion (fig. 13.7). Precise identification of this problem by means of the shot results alone is not possible, because the shots are so widely scattered.

Correction: The correction can be undertaken by the archer on his own, by trying to feel the placement of the flap of the hakama against his back; or it can be done with the help of another archer, who watches for correct placement of the hakama no kushita. A slight hollowing of the lower back is of course necessary; the pelvis

FIGURE 13.8

should be positioned slightly forward at the top and rearward at the bottom so that the buttocks protrude slightly.

Mistakes in Posture

9. The whole body is leaning too far backward.
This fault has three causes:

- The position of the pelvis is wrong, resulting in the whole body leaning backward (fig. 13.8).
- The rib cage is pushed too far forward.
- Because of bad head posture, the upper body is thrown out of position.

Shot result: For the most part, arrows go behind the mato. This mistake often arises during yugamae or else in the moment at which the draw begins, when as a result of the effort, the upper body is thrown backward as a counterweight to the force of the pull.

Correction: One should pay attention to keeping the chest muscles relaxed and should let neither the abdomen nor the chest come too far forward. One succeeds at this more easily if one makes an effort to keep the back straight and extended. In case this mistake comes about from dozukuri, of course one has to go back and execute dozukuri properly.

10. The body is leaning too far forward, because either the upper body is bent too far forward (fig. 13.9) or else the pelvis is pushed too far back (fig. 13.10).

Shot result: Arrows go either in front of or under the mato.

Correction: The musculature of the pelvis has to be strengthened, and dozukuri has to be precisely executed and then maintained. Of course, in the early practice of dozukuri, one has to be careful that the spine does not develop too strong an S-curve. Some schools pay little attention to this excessive curvature of the backbone and permit their students to take this posture.

FIGURE 13.9   FIGURE 13.10

Figure 13.11

Even disregarding the fact that this is not a very elegant external form, this spinal sag has a bad effect in nobiai, as a rule causing arrows to fly short.

11. The upper body is leaning toward the target, that is, to the left.

This problem develops in yugamae or else at the beginning of the draw (fig. 13.11). A further cause is that the Heki Ryu performs yugamae in a leftward position. In the styles of other schools, this problem does not come about until the draw, that is, *daisan*.

Shot result: Arrows go either in front of or over the mato. Because the left side of the body is tilted downward, naturally the bow hand is also too low and the right hand too high. Many archers under these circumstances try to balance out this bad positioning by jerking the arrow upward during hanare.

Correction: To eliminate this fault, one must assume a somewhat wider ashibumi and pay special attention to getting solid and correct positioning of the pelvis.

12. The upper body is tilted to the right (fig. 13.12).

This fault usually appears when, at the beginning of the draw, the right hand pulls too strongly, and with this pulling movement the upper body also tilts to the right.

Shot result: Arrows go over the mato.

This fault brings about others. Because arrows fly too high, the archer will often jerk the yunde (bow hand) downward by way of compensation.

Correction: If the problem appears at the beginning of the draw, then one has to make sure that the balance between the left and right hand is developing properly. If the left hand—especially at the beginning—is weaker than the right, then the left hand must definitely be strengthened. Under no circumstances should the right hand be weakened to achieve the balance. If the mistake occurs during uchiokoshi—that is, if the bow is not raised precisely by the right hand—at this point one should go back and check dozukuri.

13. The whole body is twisted.

This mistake often appears for an archer of the Heki Ryu at the moment of raising the bow during uchiokoshi. In the other schools, this mistake is often not observed until daisan (fig. 13.13).

Shot result: The direction of the arrows is dependent on the direction in which the body is twisted. It is of course also possible for arrows to go off in the opposite direction, since the infelicitous positioning of the body destroys the balance of forces, and this leads to reflexive compensatory movements at the moment of releasing the shot. These can become too pronounced and send the arrow off in the opposite direction.

Correction: Regardless of the school the archer is part of, it is important for dozukuri to be maintained while the bow is raised and during the beginning of the draw. With beginners, one should take care that the execution of yugamae does not lead to a loss of proper positioning of the upper body and the pelvis, since

FIGURE 13.12   FIGURE 13.13

torikake and tenouchi are often accomplished by the beginner
with large movements of the arms and shoulders.

MISTAKES IN YUGAMAE (14–23)

14. The left shoulder is too low and is without force.

Since in the Heki Ryu yugamae is executed off to the left side,
it easily happens that the left shoulder is brought too far backward
or slumps down to the left (fig. 13.14). If in the yugamae a very
narrow triangle develops between the arms and the trunk (when
looked at from above), this is a bad position. The view from the
top should show a trapezoid with the big end to the left.

But if the top view yields a narrow triangle, the result will be
difficulties in drawing the bow.

Shot result: This position error does not have an immediate influence on the shot. But it ends up affecting the draw in such a

FIGURE 13.14

way that arrows usually fly without force and not very far, since the bow cannot be drawn to the required level of tension.

Correction: The whole position of the upper body, the shoulders, the arms, and the wrists has to be corrected. Special attention must be paid to making sure the shoulders are set solidly and are parallel to the ashibumi. During uchiokoshi, which is coming next, one must again make sure that the shoulders are not twisted out of position to the rear.

15. Bad bow position.

If in yugamae the bow is held too far to the left, this usually has consequences for the tenouchi, since the left wrist has to make up for this by bending either inward or outward, and thus an unhindered transference of force can no longer be achieved. If the bow is quite far over to the left, then the right hand often has to be bent to compensate for this, and this leads to a serious problem, because one loses torikake.

Shot result: If the wrist is bent outward, arrows go in front of the mato, since the left hand does not have enough force for its pushing and turning. However, the arrow can also go behind the mato, because a compensatory movement of the right hand may jerk the arrow in this direction.

Correction: One must take care that the right hand makes a proper torikake and that the wrist is not bent. At the same time, one must be sure that the left hand does a proper job with tenouchi and tsunomi.

16. In doing tenouchi, the hand is pushed too far downward.

It is important for the shot for the left hand to be able to push forcefully downward during the release. But if the hand is already placed in this position during yugamae, it is an error (see also mistake #60 and fig. 13.29).

Shot result: Arrows fly off in a very scattered fashion, since the tsunomi is not able to perform its function effectively.

Correction: The hand should be positioned somewhat higher and care taken that during hanare, its downward push is properly executed. When the tsunomi is applied badly, it is also difficult to execute the necessary movement of turning the bow.

17. The wrist is positioned too far upward.

This fault occurs frequently with beginners, especially when they are using bows that are too strong for them (see also mistake #61 and fig. 13.30).

Shot result: Arrows go in front of the mato.

Correction: First one should correct the position of the wrist. Then, during the draw, one must make sure that the tsunomi is not lost. The archer must also make an effort at the release to turn the right edge of the bow forcefully and quickly in the direction of the target and to push in the proper way.

18. The left wrist is bent too far toward the back of the hand.

This mistake is also one that comes up frequently with beginners when they use too strong a bow. The observer will notice that the inside of the archer's wrist protrudes very far forward. (See also mistake #58 and fig. 13.28.)

Shot result: Arrows go in front of and under the mato. Arrows often waggle in flight, and the bowstring can easily strike the wrist or the face, since the bow cannot be properly turned.

Correction: Proper execution of tenouchi is the best means for dealing with this mistake.

19. The left wrist is bent too far toward the inside of the hand. Often this phenomenon is also the result of too strong a bow. (See also mistake #59 and fig. 13.27.)

Shot result: Since in this position the tenouchi is unsure or hardly there at all, the bow ends up being handled in quite different ways, and shots go off in a very scattered fashion. Here, too, it can occur that the bowstring strikes the hand, the forearm, or the face. The only correction is learning to execute tenouchi properly.

Mistakes in Torikake

20. The thumb points downward (fig. 13.15).

If the bow is drawn while the thumb is in this position, it frequently occurs that between sanbun no ni and tsumeai, the arrow falls off the left hand. At the time of hanare, with this thumb position it is very difficult to release the bowstring, with the result that a movement of the *mette* (right hand) in the direction of the target becomes necessary in order to release the arrow at all. This always means losing the tension on the bow that has been reached by this point, and it is therefore an error.

Correction: In performing torikake, one must take care that the thumb is at a right angle to the bowstring and that, as a result, the wrist remains relaxed and this position is not lost during the draw.

21. The thumb points up (fig. 13.16).

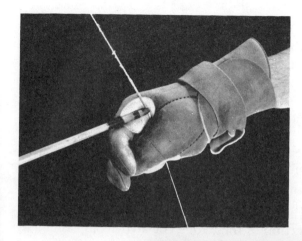

FIGURE 13.15

FIGURE 13.16

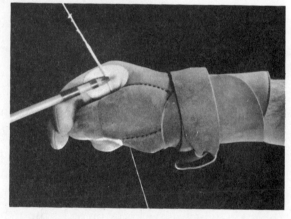

If the thumb is too high, during the phase between tsumeai and nobiai, *karahazu* might occur. That means that the arrow falls to the ground and that at the moment of releasing the bow, the release takes place without an arrow. In this circumstance, the bow might well break. However, if the arrow does stay on the string, in order to be able to bring about the release at all, a part of the tension of the draw has to be given back, and the right hand has to be moved in the direction of the target at the time of hanare.

Correction: Learning torikake properly leads with certainty to the desired result.

22. Wrong head posture in executing monomi.

The posture of the head in monomi is wrong if the head is turned or bent too far in the direction of the target. The prerequisite for correct head posture is a good dozukuri. It is impossible to come up with a definite rule for the position of the head in monomi, because this depends on individual characteristics such as the shape of the head and the position of the neck. Every archer has to find out for himself in the course of practice what his optimal head posture is in monomi. Of course, it must be free of excessive tension, so that, for example, if someone calls out to the archer from the direction of the target, the archer can easily and naturally move his head toward the caller.

Shot result: If the chin is turned too far over the shoulder, arrows go behind the mato. If the chin is too far to the right, arrows go in front of the mato.

Correction: Problems in monomi are very hard to correct, since the individual differences mentioned above make it impossible to give a definitive description of the proper posture. Nonetheless special attention must be paid to this point, particularly in mato shooting, for otherwise it is very difficult to hit the target. This is conditioned by varying placements of the arrow against the cheek (hozuke), which as we know provides the archer with feedback regarding the height of his right hand.

23. Weak neck musculature.

In this mistake, although the head is correct during monomi, during hanare the head flops around, since the neck muscles are incapable of holding it in its original position. Though this mistake does not have an immediate effect on where the shot goes, it does cause arrows to fly rather weakly.

This mistake also appears when one's mental attitude slackens and the bow is not drawn with full physical and mental force from tsumeai to nobiai. The correction is for the archer to make an effort to maintain the appropriate physical and mental tension from the beginning of the shot until its release.

MISTAKES IN UCHIOKOSHI (24–27)

24. The arrow is pointed upward.

This mistake is brought about primarily by the left hand playing too great a part in the raising of the bow (fig. 13.17). This error has no effect on where the shot goes.

Correction: The archer has to try to raise the bow almost with the right hand alone while imagining that he is very slowly and evenly lifting a weight with the right hand only.

25. The bow is not perpendicular.

This fault takes the form of the upper bow tip being too far over the archer (fig, 13.18) or of the lower tip of the bow being too near the archer's body.

Figure 13.17

Figure 13.18

Shot result: If the lower tip is too near the archer, arrows go in front of and under the mato. If the upper tip is too far over the archer, arrows go behind and above the mato.

Correction: The archer has to make sure in raising and drawing the bow that the bow remains perpendicular. It is all right, however, if the lower bow tip is a little bit tilted toward the archer. There is an exception to this correction that relates to enteki, distance shooting. In enteki, the lower bow tip can at this point be farther from the archer than in other forms of shooting.

Breathing and Timing

26. Uchiokoshi is too fast.

Raising the bow should be coordinated with the breath. If the archer inhales too fast, as a rule he also raises the bow very fast. The reverse is true as well.

This mistake has no influence on the shot result, unless, as a consequence of breathing too shallowly, the archer runs out of breath in nobiai and is unable to stretch the bow forcefully and long enough. The raising of the bow should take place in three phases. First the bow is slowly and calmly disengaged from the knee; the main phase is of course carried out with fluid speed; and the last part of the raising is once again very slow and calm.

27. Uchiokoshi is too slow.

This mistake also is often due to wrong breathing. The archer must take care that the breathing and the raising of the bow are coordinated.

Although this mistake has no influence on the shot result, breathing errors might continue into the archer's further movements as the shot continues. In this case, it is important for the archer to pay attention to proper management of the breath.

MISTAKES IN HIKIWAKE
(SANBUN NO NI) (28–45)

Drawing and Posture Problems in Sanbun No Ni

28. In beginning to draw the bow, the right hand pulls too hard.

The shot result is not directly influenced by this mistake. However, the archer must make an effort to initiate the drawing of the bow with the left hand; that is, first the left hand pushes, then the right hand follows by pulling. In this mistake the arrow is often too high on the left end (fig. 13.19).

29. Sanbun no ni is too small.

In this mistake, the right hand ends up in front of the ear. In consequence, as the shot continues it is impossible to achieve an adequately full draw, and arrows go off very weakly. In addition,

FIGURE 13.19

FIGURE 13.20   FIGURE 13.21

there can be difficulties with hanare, since the arrow cannot be properly released from the glove (fig. 13.20).

Correction: The archer must work to achieve a proper sanbun no ni; that is, the right hand must be behind the ear. He must bring the right elbow far enough back, and the left hand has to push in the direction of the target with comparatively equal force.

30. Sanbun no ni is too big.

In this mistake, the right hand comes too far back behind the head and ear (fig. 13.21). The consequence is that one cannot draw the bow any further for the kai, and either simply lowers the arrow for tsumeai or else does indeed draw the bow wider, but then is forced to bend the right wrist quite far, which represents a further serious error.

Correction: The archer must execute sanbun no ni with proper form and must especially strengthen his tsunomi and his right elbow.

31. Sanbun no ni is too high.

Although it is permissible to execute sanbun no ni at somewhat higher than eyebrow level, if the arrow is significantly above the eyebrows, this often brings disadvantages for the further draw, and shots go off weakly (fig. 13.22).

Correction: One should execute the draw slowly and calmly until one has reached the correct position for sanbun no ni.

32. Sanbun no ni is too low (fig. 13.23).

In the basic form of the Heki Ryu, hozuke (the placement of the arrow against the cheek) is a decisive point for the correct form of the shot. If sanbun no ni is too low, hozuke cannot be done properly, and the archer has difficulties with the release, and also the stretching of the bow that comes before that will be difficult. This fault is also called hayake. This means a release that is too quick or premature, that happens without the necessary physical and mental heightening of tension.

FIGURE 13.22   FIGURE 13.23

Correction: The student must come to a clear understanding of a proper sanbun no ni and try to execute it correctly as part of his basic form.

Mistakes in Balances of Force in Sanbun No Ni

33. The right hand is stronger than the left hand.

This fault can obviously also come up the other way around, with the left hand stronger than the right. However, the latter fault is rather rare, since most people are right-handed and therefore have more force and sense of movement in their right hand. Since, however, in kyudo the left hand leads in drawing the bow and also must work with strength and precision at the time of releasing the shot, a strong left hand is never a disadvantage.

Shot result: If the right hand is too strong, arrows go in front of the mato.

Correction: One must make an effort over time to make the left hand stronger than the right and in this way redress the balance. It is not helpful to weaken the right hand to get the left hand to be stronger by comparison.

It has been discovered from special photographs and measurements that good archers shoot with a ratio of force of two-thirds left and one-third right. This corresponds to historical traditions.

34. In drawing the bow, the left hand pushes too fast.

The archer should be aware that in drawing the bow, the left hand and the right hand have to cover distances of different lengths in the same time. If the left hand moves too fast, the archer is already aiming when the right hand has not yet finished its move, and again this leads to hayake.

Another effect might be that the arrow is not shot horizontally but goes off in a downward direction.

Shot result: Arrows often go either in front of or behind the mato.

Correction: As already mentioned, a strong left hand is no disadvantage. But the archer must work toward a balanced coordination of both hands at the beginning of the draw as well as attempt to improve it during the sanbun no ni and maintain it until the moment of release.

Movement Mistakes in Sanbun no Ni

35. Pausing in sanbun no ni.

If one tries to hold on to one's force for a moment rather than maintain the tension as though in an endless slow draw, then, as one's movements continue, one is obliged to come up with new force. One then has to call on other muscles for help, resulting in unnecessary and wrong movements, especially in the shoulders. Since sanbun no ni is the preparation for tsumeai and nobiai, one should not interrupt the flow of force at this point but must steadily, though very slowly, carry it through.

36. Uneven movement in the draw.

Although it crops up relatively rarely, some archers do not draw the bow evenly but by jerks, or else they pause several times in the course of the draw. This is often due to bad coordination of breath and movement.

In uchiokoshi, ideally the archer should breathe in and begin to breathe out as he starts drawing the bow. There should be no further new breaths until the shot is released. However, beginners find it impossible to carry out the entire shot on one breath. They, especially, must pay attention to the alternation of inhalation and exhalation, so that no interruption of the flow of movement occurs in the course of the draw.

37. Mistakes in drawing the bow.
   a. The bow is drawn almost over the head.
   b. The hands are far from the body, and the draw takes place with the bow almost on the horizontal.
   c. The movement is carried out directly at the face.
   d. The archer first assumes the position of hozuke and then produces extra tension on the bow through backward motion of the arms.

EFFECTS
- At hanare, both hands are jerked downward.
- There is an optimal series of movements leading to hanare, which this error in form renders impossible, since the left hand has to push too hard and after hanare is often flung backward.
- The movement in the direction of the face causes the force of the right hand to predominate. Overburdening the right side often brings the left shoulder too far forward, tsunomi is lost, and hanare becomes weak and small.
- The effectiveness of tsunomi is either weakened or lost. Hanare happens too soon, sometimes while the draw is still in progress.

Correction: The archer has to train with dedication in the basic form. He must return again to precise practice either with a very light bow or else with the rubber practice bow, paying special attention to the proper balance of force between the right and left hands.

Mistakes in the Movement of the Shoulders

38. The left shoulder is too high.
This mistake usually appears when the archer is using too strong a bow, but it also occurs with people who carry their shoulder very high as a result of a mistake in posture. The con-

sequence of this very bad posture is that in the hanare the shoulders are jerked upward or else movements made to counter this appear.

Correction: The correction of this mistake requires a long time and should not happen too fast. The archer can do the following exercise to get the sense of the correct shoulder position: He stands by a wall or pillar with the left arm and hand stretched out and pushes on the wall as he would on the bow, observing how the left shoulder is pushed down and also, in the case of a hard push, stays down. After that, the archer should try to come to this same feeling again in working with a bow. However, if this posture mistake stems from a characteristic of the archer's constitution, he must make his ashibumi somewhat wider and try as hard as he can to keep his shoulders low.

39. The left shoulder is too far back.

In this mistake, the line between the hands, elbows, and shoulders is broken. The left shoulder protrudes too far back. This mistake is frequently the result of a bad yugamae, which is done off to the left side in the Heki Ryu. Then during the draw, because of the burden it is under, the left shoulder is driven yet further back.

Correction: The archer has to take care during yugamae to keep his shoulders parallel to the shooting line, not to twist them out of place during uchiokoshi, and to consciously bring them forward and down during the draw. Frequently it happens that in correcting his shoulders, the archer loses his tenouchi. Of course, this cannot be allowed to happen, so he must pay attention to both his shoulders and his hands.

40. The right shoulder is too high.

This mistake, too, is often caused by too strong a bow. As a result, with the beginning of the draw, the right shoulder often goes up and the right elbow too far down. This is another mistake that may be caused by constitutional characteristics of the archer.

Correction: In beginning to draw the bow, the archer must be aware in advance of the position of his shoulders and correct it if necessary. In the course of the draw, he must make an effort to make his right shoulder stay down and pay special attention to his right elbow as the leading point in the pull.

41. The right shoulder is too far forward.
When, in drawing, one brings the right elbow too far to the rear, the right shoulder is pushed forward by way of compensation. As a result, the draw begins with the balance of force too strongly on the right side, which leads to weak shots. Likewise, in nobiai one ends up with an elbow position that is not optimal.

Shot result: For the reasons mentioned, arrows fly in a very scattered fashion.

Correction: The archer must pay special attention to the position of both shoulders and, during the draw, bring the right elbow toward the rear in a big, broad movement. The archer should have the feeling that at hanare he is going to bang his elbows against something.

Mistakes in Elbow Movements

42. (a) The left elbow is too high and the left wrist is pushed down. (b) The left elbow is too low and the left wrist is pushed up.

Correction: These outward appearances often come about as a result of constitutional characteristics of the archer. Therefore, correction based on the outward form is very difficult. For this reason the archer must try hard to pay attention to the balance between the arms and try to bring this about regardless of how the outer form looks. In such a case, it might be necessary to alter the tenouchi within the acceptable range of deviation.

43. The force used in drawing the bow is not developed from the right elbow but rather from the wrist.

This fault is very frequently seen in beginners.

Shot result: Shots fly in an extremely scattered fashion.

Correction: An advanced archer or a teacher takes hold of the archer's wrist and moves it the way it should move, making sure that no tension develops in the wrist. This should be continued until the archer masters a proper draw, which must come exclusively from the upper arm. In addition, it is helpful to have the student execute the movement without a bow, that is, just in the air, or else with the rubber practice bow, before he returns once again to practicing with a bow and arrow.

44. Loss of a proper torikake.

Even when torikake is executed in the prescribed manner, in order to keep the arrow from falling, the archer is compelled to develop a certain tension in the right wrist during the draw. But at the beginning of the draw, putting a great deal of force in the right hand is not necessary. If the right hand, particularly the wrist, is too tense, this leads to the following faults:

a. The wrist is bent downward.
b. The wrist is positioned too low, and the thumb points upward.
c. During the draw, the turning action that holds the arrow is given up.

Shot result: If the arrow does not fall off the left hand or out of the right hand, shots end up quite short, that is, in front of the mato. A further consequence is that in hanare the archer gives back tension at the moment of releasing the shot.

Correction: One must be sure to achieve a correct torikake in which the arrow is securely but not too strongly held. The necessary tension in the right wrist must be held constant all the way to the release.

Tenouchi and the Balance of Force between the Hands

45. The balance of force between the left and right hands during tsumeai is very vulnerable to being upset. If one draws only with the right wrist, the left hand becomes relatively too weak at the time of kai.

Correction: The archer must already feel the required balance of two-thirds force in the left hand and one-third force in the right at the time of yugamae and then continue it until the end of the shot.

MISTAKES IN TSUMEAI (46–51)

46. The bow is drawn too far.

In this mistake the right hand comes back too far behind the head. The wrist is bent, and the right hand frequently cannot be turned far enough inward to keep a hold on the arrow. Since with the wrist bent and without this inward turn, the arrow cannot be released properly, as a rule the archer lets up on the tension of the bow or else opens his hand. This results in arrows being shot weakly and as a rule under the mato.

Correction: After a correct sanbun no ni, the archer must draw the bow in the right way with his elbow and steadily continue to turn the right hand inward. This fault can also arise when an archer uses a bow that is much too weak for him and that he can therefore overdraw without effort. In this case, it is advisable to switch to a stronger bow. The length of the draw should not be greater than half the archer's height.

47. The bow is not drawn far enough.

When at tsumeai, the bow is not drawn far enough, the balance in the shoulders is also lost. The left shoulder often shifts backward or the right shoulder forward, or perhaps the right elbow protrudes forward.

Shot result: Shots are weak, and the string readily strikes the left forearm. The string hitting the forearm or the wrist is often caused by a bad tenouchi, a mistake that follows from the inadequate tension in the bow; such a tenouchi is no longer capable of providing an effective transfer of force to the bow when it comes to pushing and turning.

Correction: The archer must consider whether the bow he is using might be too strong and whether that is the reason why he is not able to draw it far enough. It might be beneficial to practice the correct position for tsumeai again with a light bow or with a rubber practice bow before returning to practice with bow, arrow, and glove.

48. Munazuru does not occur.

This means that the bow no longer has contact with the body; that is, the string (*tsuru*) does not touch the chest. Since in this position the bow easily wobbles around, the resulting shots are scattered.

Shot result: Shots go either in front of or behind the mato.

Correction: This mistake might arise because the bow is not drawn far enough or because the turning of the hands is too slight. One must determine its cause before correcting it.

49. Hozuke is too high.

This mistake is common among beginners who have yet to develop the right sense of movement in drawing the bow and therefore bring the bow close to the body too soon; this results in the arrow touching the face too high (fig. 13.24).

50. Hozuke is too low.

This mistake is a frequent one among older archers or people using a bow that does not suit their strength (fig. 13.25).

FIGURE 13.24   FIGURE 13.25

Shot result: Shots are weak and thus often go under the mato.

Correction: The archer must pay attention to whether the correct balance is present between the left and right sides of the body, and then continue with tension distributed equally to both sides. Drawing too low with the right hand often has the consequence that hanare can only be executed with great difficulty. Thus hanare must also be looked at in connection with this mistake.

51. Aiming mistake resulting from a disturbance in balance.

This mistake can easily be uncovered in the following way. If the archer's shots hit the target, but a second person, standing behind the archer during nobiai, sights down his arrow at the target and sees that actually the arrow should not be hitting the target at all, then this is an aiming error.

Correction: The second person, who is observing the archer, has to correct his aim. If the archer has the arrow directed too far in front of the mato—that is, if he is aiming to the right—this aiming mistake is usually compensated for during hanare by the archer's jerking his left hand sharply back and to the left at the moment of release, or by moving his right hand back toward the bow. But if during aiming the arrow is directed too far behind the target, the archer often compensates for this by executing an overly weak hanare to the left or one that is too strong to the right.

MISTAKES IN NOBIAI (52–56)

52. Disturbance of the balance of forces in drawing the bow and in breathing during nobiai.

In the drawing of the bow, nobiai is one of the most important moments before the release of the shot. Thus it is easy to understand that especially at this point an exact balance of forces and good breath control must be present. If the balance of forces in completing the draw and in-breathing is disturbed, three shooting mistakes arise:

a. Hayake: Premature release of the shot.
b. Busuki: Shooting without pleasure or interest, with absence of force in posture and in mental attitude.
c. Chijimi: Giving back some of the tension in the bow with the right arm at the time of the hanare. Shots are weak, cramped, and half-hearted.

Hayake

These three mistakes are altogether the most serious ones that can occur in the course of shooting, and hayake is the most serious of the three. These mistakes are therefore also very difficult to correct. The overall picture of the mistake is that the process of drawing from nobiai to yagoro is not continued, but instead the shot is prematurely released. This is even more serious when the process of the draw does not reach hozuke (cheek contact), but the shot is already released while the right hand is still in front of the face.

Shot result: Since the requisite extension of the draw is not fully achieved, or the placement of the arrow on the cheek is lacking, ones ends up with very scattered shots.

Correction: To combat hayake effectively, it is advisable to begin to practice with a light bow. To work with this mistake, the archer should be fully free of mental inhibitions such as are caused by being overly conscious of the target. Therefore, it is a good idea for him not to shoot at the mato but only at the makiwara.

After this fault has been eliminated at the makiwara, the archer should once again shoot at the mato. At that point, attention should be paid to getting the basic shooting technique right and little regard given to whether or not the arrow hits the target.

Another possible cause of this mistake might be that the archer has wrong ideas about aiming and hitting the target. He should therefore try to execute the basic technique consistently and to improve it without regard to hitting the target. The result will be that, over time, arrows will concentrate more and more in the direction of the target and begin to strike home. Since hayake is the most serious mistake in shooting, one must correct it as soon as it is noticed, bringing to bear all the force and discipline one can muster in dealing with it.

53. Yurumi.

In this fault, although hozuke takes place and the draw is correctly carried out up to that point, immediately before hanare, the right arm lets up and moves in the direction of the target in order to release the arrow. This brings about a loss in the tension of the draw that has been achieved up to that point, and shots are significantly weaker.

Correction: Here too it is beneficial for the archer to use a lighter bow than he has been using. In shooting he must pay attention to achieving an even execution of the draw up to hanare. Thus he must not interrupt the draw or trigger hanare intentionally, but rather let it come about through the steady continuation of the drawing process.

A further cause of this mistake might be that the archer has yet to understand the significance and function of tsunomi in the release.

54. Chijimi.

The general picture of this mistake is similar to that of yurumi. The difference is that in yurumi, at the moment of hanare the right arm lets up and moves in the direction of the target, whereas in chijimi the letup on the tension of the draw comes during tsumeai, and the draw is on the whole small and half-hearted.

Shot result: Shots are very weak and almost always far under the mato. They express the fact that the archer has shot without concentration and mental tension. The Japanese also say in this connection that through letting up on the tension in the bow, kyudo has "died."

When chijimi appears alone as a mistake and the left hand is comparatively quite weak, it can happen that shots strike the mato anyway. Despite this result, because of bad balance and lack of tension in the draw, we speak of a shooting mistake.

Because the arrows hit the target, this mistake can be very difficult to uncover. However, once it has been detected, it must be strictly and strenuously corrected.

Correction: The archer should shoot with a light bow and continually say to himself that he has not drawn far enough and can draw farther. In the context of this correction, it is important for the archer to come to understand the right timing of hanare and the function of tsunomi. Here again it is true: the left hand must lead, the right hand follow.

55. The upper body leans toward the target.

This mistake occurs when the archer attempts to draw and control the bow only with the left hand. The right side of the body does not participate in a balanced fashion in drawing the bow, and the left hand alone determines hanare, which as a consequence happens too late. After the release of the shot, the body frequently leans over in the direction of the target or easily ends up swaying back and forth.

Shot result: Shots go either under or behind and under the mato.

Correction: After uchiokoshi, one must pay attention to the proper balance of the shoulders and arms. During the draw, in particular during nobiai, one must take care to preserve the balance and to make sure that hanare does not proceed from the left hand alone. The archer should have the feeling that hanare is proceeding from the middle of the body. This mistake frequently appears when the archer tries to release the shot from the left side. His exertion then makes the left hand relatively too strong. As has been pointed out already, it is no fault for the left hand to be forceful and strong. But the force in the right elbow must be strong enough to create a proper balance with the force on the left side of the body.

56. The upper body leans to the right.

This error frequently occurs after sanbun no ni when the archer is trying very hard to draw the bow farther than he has until now. In this effort, the right arm easily gets pulled back too far, and the upper body shifts to the right. In that case, the tip of the arrow often ends up too high (fig. 13.26).

Shot result: Shots go in front of and over the mato.

FIGURE 13.26

The correction for this has already been described in relation to mistake #55; here it must be applied in a corresponding fashion to the opposite side.

MISTAKES IN HANARE (57–83)

Yunde and Tsunomi

57. Imprecise Tenouchi

Tsunomi cannot function properly during hanare if tenouchi is already badly formed during yugamae. The archer must therefore make the effort to execute tenouchi correctly during this phase and must not allow himself to think that it is impossible for him to hold the bow in the manner prescribed by tradition.

The work of the bow hand during the release is of particular importance, and the transference of force through the grip must be accomplished in the right way, since mistakes due to negligence in the preceding hassetsu will have an unfavorable effect on the shot result at this point.

58. The wrist is bent inward.

This mistake frequently appears already during yugamae (see mistake #18) if the bow is not moved far enough to the left but is held too strongly by the bow hand in front of the middle of the body (fig. 13.27).

Correction: The archer must take care during yugamae that tsunomi is correctly applied.

59. The wrist is bent outward.

This is practically the opposite of mistake #58. This mistake, too, can make its appearance during yugamae if one applies tenouchi (mistake #19) too far to the right on the bow or else if the tsunomi is not strong enough and shifts as the draw develops. Since as a result of the wrist's being strongly bent out to the right, no transference of force onto the bow can take place, at the release the string often strikes the forearm or the wrist (fig. 13.28).

Shot result: Shots go in front of and under the mato.

Correction: The archer must apply tenouchi properly and keep it that way throughout the shot. If the mistake is caused by the tsunomi's shifting during the draw, the archer must make an effort to increase the force in his fingers. It would be ideal if an archer were able to develop a force of 40 kilograms in his grip. This can be achieved if the archer does not change too fast from a weak to a strong bow, but slowly increases the level of pull he has to deal with.

60. The wrist is bent too far downward (fig. 13.29).

In this error, the entire hand is inclined too far toward the little-finger side. This fault frequently occurs when the archer tries

FIGURE 13.27

FIGURE 13.28

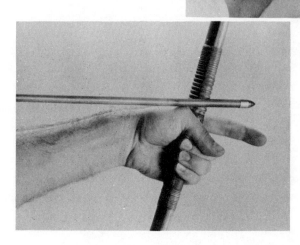

FIGURE 13.29

very hard to push with the left hand. It occurs predominantly with older archers. After the release of the shot, the bow frequently swings back and forth, and the release occurs too late. Arrows fly low and slow, and the overall shot result is bad.

Correction: Here, too, correction begins with proper application of tenouchi and the tsunomi (see also mistake #16).

61. The wrist is bent too far upward (fig. 13.30).

In this error the wrist is pushed up too far toward the thumb side of the hand. This form can frequently be observed in beginners who are using a bow that is too strong for them, with the result that the bow bends the wrist as described. Since the tsunomi is not correct and the transference of force to the bow cannot be adequately carried through, at the release the string frequently hits the forearm or the wrist.

Shot result: Shots are widely scattered and very rarely hit the target.

Correction: Tenouchi must be painstakingly executed, and during aiming, the force in the tsunomi must increase in the same measure as the force employed overall for the drawing of the bow.

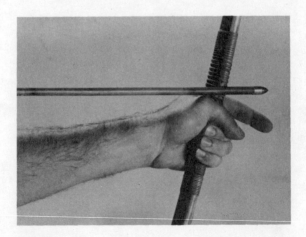

FIGURE 13.30

This mistake can be worked on in a particular way: During yugamae, the bow can be drawn only on the tsunomi—that is, laid on the V-shaped forked hand and drawn with the hand open, so that the point of pressure can really be felt and experienced (see mistake #17).

Mistakes in Movements of the Left Shoulder

62. (a) The left shoulder is too high. (b) The left shoulder slumps backward.

Both these errors are caused either by a bad yugamae, in which the left shoulder is already held toward the back and this mistake then continues through uchiokoshi into the draw; or else by the fact that the bow is too strong for the archer, who is thus not able to hold the shoulder in the correct posture while shooting.

Correction: The archer should practice with a lighter bow and execute the form properly. Once the form can be executed correctly with a light bow, the archer should slowly increase the strength of his bow until he can execute the shot with a heavy bow.

63. The left shoulder is too low.

This mistake seldom occurs. It is mostly a result of the archer's constitution.

Shot result: Shots go over the mato.

Correction: The archer must make an effort to keep his right shoulder as low as the left. If the left shoulder is only slightly lower, this fault can be compensated for by taking a somewhat narrower ashibumi.

64. The left shoulder is too far forward.

This mistake also occurs only very rarely. As a result of this posture, during hanare the shoulder moves back, and during zanshin the yunde (bow hand) moves. If this posture is present during aiming, it can also have later effects, because the bow cannot be held correctly and this can easily lead to shakiness in the left shoulder and in the yunde.

Correction: The archer must take care to position the right shoulder in proper balance to the left. He should make sure that the lines between the feet in ashibumi and between the shoulders and the arrow all run parallel.

Improper, Intentionally Produced Turning of the Bow after the Shot

Yugaeri, the turning of the bow after hanare, should come about in a totally natural fashion. Many archers, however, bring about this movement intentionally by opening the tenouchi or by making a swerving movement with the wrist that spins the bow around.

If tenouchi and tsunomi are strong, yugaeri occurs quite naturally, and one does not need to bring this result about through incorrect and superfluous movements.

65. Improper yugaeri brought about by throwing back the wrist.

When an archer attempts to produce yugaeri by throwing back the wrist, he usually loses his tenouchi and opens his hand after hanare. As a result, shots are weak and widely scattered.

Correction: The archer should not think about yugaeri or bring it about intentionally, but just make his tenouchi strong and keep it that way until the end of the shot.

66. Improper yugaeri produced by opening the bow hand (fig. 13.31).

This error is often found in older kyudoka. Since the tsunomi and tenouchi are completely lost by opening the hand, shots are quite weak and usually go in front of the mato. Yugaeri takes place too late and too slowly. The bow slips down through the hand and is in the wrong position after the release of the shot. For this

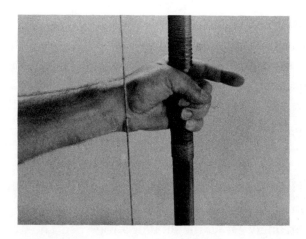

FIGURE 13.31

reason, the string often strikes against the bow and makes a very loud noise. It is true that there is always some sound from the string when the arrow is released, but the right *tsurune* (sound of the string at the release of the shot) has a much sharper sound.

Correction: The archer must in no way bring about yugaeri intentionally and must give special attention to keeping the tenouchi correct until the end of the shot. Attention should not be directed toward the turning of the bow but should be placed primarily on correctly pushing and turning.

67. The midpoint for turning the bow is in the wrong place.

The bow should properly turn around its front left corner. The mistake consists in the archer's attempting to turn the bow around its front right corner.

Shot result: Shots go in front of and under the mato, since at the release of the shot, the left hand is moved forward rather than backward.

Correction: During the draw, especially in the last part of kai, the archer must lean entirely into the bow and try to stretch the yunde, especially at the pulse point on the inside of the wrist, in the direction of the mato.

68. At hanare the arms move upward.

In this mistake, the arms move simultaneously upward and forward, so that the hands end up in front of the line of the shoulders. This error often has the same appearance as mistake #65.

Shot result: Shots go over and in front of the mato, and the bowstring hits the wrist.

Correction: In drawing the bow, the archer must take care to:

    a. Hold the back straight and be clearly aware of the tension in the back muscles.

    b. Strongly gather the shoulders together. The archer should make an effort to get the shoulder blades to touch in the middle.

69. The left hand is thrust too strongly in the direction of the mato.

As a consequence of this, the upper body, too, leans over left toward the target. Because at the release of the shot, the left hand with the releasing arrow is also thrust too strongly in the direction of the target, the release loses force, and the arrow flies very weakly. However, only a slight manifestation of this mistake may not alter the shot result.

Correction: The archer must take care to maintain a straight body position throughout the entire shot and to keep the right balance of force between the left and right hands during the release of the shot.

Mistakes in Movement of the Right Hand during Hanare

70. The right hand is opened during hanare.

This mistake is very difficult to correct. The archer must virtually relearn the movement of the right hand from the beginning.

If one opens the right hand intentionally in order to make the release, then the force of the right elbow is completely lost. Moreover, this form in hanare is lacking in elegance.

It is not necessary to bring about hanare intentionally by opening the right hand. Slow-motion film has proved that hanare takes place even if the thumb remains in definite contact with the middle and ring fingers.

71. During hanare, the right hand moves back in the direction of the mato.

This mistake arises when the effort of drawing is carried out too much with the right side of the body, or else when the right wrist is bent during the draw in such a way that the necessary inward turn can no longer be executed. In order for the archer to be able to turn his wrist, he has to interrupt his pull and reduce the tension of the draw.

Shot result: Shots go behind and under the mato.

Correction: The archer must take care to carry out the drawing of the bow exclusively through the force of his right elbow and to keep his wrist relaxed. One can also practice the inward turn needed to fix the arrow in place in order to get rid of this mistake.

72. During hanare the right elbow is moved back in the direction of the mato.

Moving the elbow back in the direction of the target can occur by moving the elbow either upward or downward in the direction of the target. By moving the elbow back toward the target, the tensing achieved up to this point is interrupted or even partially given up; as a result, arrows fly weakly and as a rule under the mato. This mistake is caused either by the archer's using too weak a bow or by his lacking in concentration—that is, shooting without the necessary mental tension.

Correction: In the first case, the archer should use a stronger bow. But if the mistake is more mental in nature, then he should concentrate on putting himself entirely into the bow and on drawing it further than he has hitherto considered possible.

During the shot, one must put oneself entirely into the bow and broaden out the chest, so that the release of the shot is really felt to come from the middle of the body.

73. Incorrect inward turning of the right wrist or failure to execute it altogether.

If the archer does not continuously turn the right hand inward during nobiai, then the tension of the draw cannot be increased, and the resulting shot is comparatively weak. Nobiai is interrupted, and frequently to bring about the release, the left arm is also moved forward, and chijimi occurs.

Shot result: Shots go in front of and under the mato.

Correction: The archer must pay attention to the entire movement of the right arm and wrist. The control and movement of the right elbow are part of this, as are the increasing of the angle between the upper arm and the forearm and the inward turning of the right hand. If the archer takes care to bring about the proper relationship of these three movements, this fault can be corrected rather quickly.

74. Use of an ill-fitting glove.

If the archer uses an inappropriate glove or a glove in which the string groove is not properly formed, this will obviously have its consequences for his shooting, especially with regard to the release. Either the string is very hard to release from the groove, or—especially with gloves that are too big—the string slips out of the groove before the bow is fully drawn, and the shot is released too soon.

The various schools and shooting styles in kyudo require differently fashioned gloves. Thus, for example, it is not advisable to use a glove meant for fast shooting or for enteki in normal mato shooting, since the release methods for these other methods are different than that employed in normal mato shooting. For the standard mato, the Heki Ryu uses a glove in which the groove for the string is almost at a right angle to the longitudinal axis of the thumb. Thus the archer must be sure that he is using a properly fashioned glove in his practice.

Hayake (Premature Release)

75. Hayake from using too strong a bow.

Hayake easily occurs when the archer is using too strong a bow, which he does not have the strength to draw fully; this results in a premature release of the arrow.

Correction consists in the use of a bow that suits the archer's strength. If, when using a very strong bow, hayake occurs only occasionally, then this is not a fault. The archer must make an effort to maintain the previously established rhythm right through hanare and not allow himself to become habituated to a premature release.

76. Hayake as a result of lack of concentration.

If one does not work with the requisite concentration up to zanshin, then—especially in the case of archers who are already somewhat advanced—hayake due to lack of concentration can easily result. Believing that one already knows shooting and has mastered it, one executes hanare automatically and almost merely as a matter of reflex. But then this lack of mindfulness and tension has the effect of making it very difficult to hit the mark. Because of successful marksmanship in the past, it becomes very difficult for the archer to recognize lack of mental tension as the cause of hayake, and thus on the whole this becomes a very difficult mistake to correct. Above all, the archer should endeavor to lengthen his nobiai and must cease executing hanare deliberately or intentionally.

It is also advisable to begin with to work on this mistake at the makiwara.

If the reason for the lack of concentration during nobiai is that the archer is concentrating too much on the target with a wish to hit it, the mistake hardly comes up at the makiwara, but then it must of course be worked on at the mato. Here the help of a teacher is practically indispensable; at the least the archer should draw on the advice of an archer as advanced as he is in working on this mistake.

77. Hayake resulting from a weak tsunomi.

If the tsunomi is too weak, the left hand has no possibility of matching the pull of the right hand with an equivalent force. In an effort to avoid this disruption of the balance between the left and right hands, the archer releases the arrow too soon, thinking that preservation of the balance is more important than a correctly executed, unintentional hanare. In this form of hayake, nobiai is frequently only one or two seconds long. Hits on the target become more or less accidental, and the overall shot result is highly scattered.

Correction: The archer must improve and strengthen his tsunomi and for the time being give up any thoughts of hitting the target.

As with the preceding mistakes, it is perhaps a good idea here also to use a lighter bow for a short time, first working in front of the makiwara and afterward again practicing at the mato. But in front of the mato, too, the archer must make an effort to shoot with correct basic form, regardless of results at the target.

78. Hayake as a result of wrong breathing.

Wrong breathing alone is seldom the cause of hayake, but this form of hayake often crops up combined with mistakes such as a bad mental attitude that is exclusively oriented toward hitting the target, or with other movement faults.

Correction: The archer must endeavor to breathe in a relaxed and uncramped manner, taking care that movements and breathing are coordinated. Although the proper rhythm for breathing can be pointed out in general terms, it cannot be systematically learned on the basis of a schema. Every archer has to find and sense his own rhythm and gently and fluidly coordinate breathing and movement.

Other Mistakes in Hanare

79. Unnecessary movements of the head during hanare.

During hanare the archer's head moves either forward and backward or from side to side. The cause is a lack of tension in the neck muscles during the release. This mistake does not have an immediate effect on the shot. However, it is defective as an external form.

Correction: This mistake can be easily eliminated by making sure that the slanting muscles of the chest are tensed during no-biai and hanare. If one shoots with full physical and mental tension, such mistakes in form can scarcely occur. They are frequently an indication that the archer is in fear of his own release and therefore makes this type of superfluous movement.

80. The upper body leans backward during hanare.

This error also often appears in combination with other mistakes. Especially when, because of a lack of force in the left hand, the string strikes the archer's face or forearm and he tries to counter this phenomenon by quickly leaning backward during the release, afraid of suffering the pain of being hit by the string yet again. Since, in this type of release, the bow is not fully drawn, shots are quite weak and often go under the target.

Correction: The archer must try to achieve correct basic form and develop the courage needed for a proper hanare. In difficult cases, it might be necessary for the archer to go back to practicing a correct hanare with the rubber practice bow for a while, until he has lost his fear of hanare. Then he can train once again with a bow and arrow.

81. Position of the arms during hanare.

When the shot is released correctly, the two hands should move apart symmetrically as viewed from the middle of the body. The shooting mistake consists in ending up after the shot with the right hand low and the left hand high, or the other way around.

a) If the left hand is moved upward after the shot is released, this can be due to incorrect aiming, and the archer is attempting to compensate for having aimed low by jerking his left hand upward at the release. If the cause of this mistake is, as described above, in the aiming, then one has to work with the archer again on aiming. He must be able to execute a correct hanare with the arrow held horizontally and to observe in nobiai how he sees the target in relation to the bow. But if shots continue to go too low despite this, one must look for another shooting error that might be responsible for it. If the archer is using a comparatively weak bow that is not capable of shooting a horizontally held arrow far enough to reach the target, then he is obliged to hold the left hand somewhat higher and not try at the moment of shooting to give the arrow a better placement angle by making a sudden movement (fig. 13.32).

b) Another movement mistake consists in jerking both hands simultaneously upward after hanare (fig. 13.33). This mistake frequently occurs when the archer has a wrong understanding of what the balance should be at the moment of the shot. Because of the constant execution of movements from above downward during the course of the draw, it can indeed be only a natural result when, after hanare, the hands continue to move downward in the same way. Frequently one encounters archers who, although they execute a proper hanare, nevertheless afterward

FIGURE 13.32   FIGURE 13.33

intentionally move both hands in a countermovement, jerking them upward. Though this no longer has an effect on the shot, it never represents a mistake in form, since zanshin will not then be a result of the forces at work up to that point. However, because it is a change in the direction of movement, it is possible that this movement in the opposite direction might already be having an effect before hanare that results in an interruption in the ongoing tensing of the bow, in shots being weak, and in the turning of the bow not taking place.

Correction: The archer must strive for correct basic technique and must study the phases of nobiai and zanshin with particular precision.

c) The right hand is too high after the shot has been released and the left too low. This error configuration represents practically the reverse of that of the first mistake (81a) mentioned above. The archer always aims too high and tries unconsciously to compensate for the mistake through additional movements (fig. 13.34).

FIGURE 13.34   FIGURE 13.35

This mistake can be corrected in the same way as mistake (a) mentioned above.

d) After the release of the shot, both hands are quite far below the shoulders. This mistake is frequently found among beginners, who intentionally try to arrive at the desired form of zanshin and thus deliberately move their hands strongly downward (fig. 13.35). This mistake has scarcely any influence on the shot, yet the student should understand in practice that a good nobiai results in a proper hanare and a natural zanshin that need not be altered by means of additional movements.

82. Distortion of facial muscles.

This phenomenon is not a shooting mistake that affects the shot results. Nonetheless it shows that the archer is making a wrong effort in executing his shot. Getting the feeling of tension necessary for a correct nobiai should be confined exclusively to the muscles needed to bring this about and not be shifted to the muscles of the face, since this creates a comical and unfavorable impression.

Correction: The archer is often not in a position himself to notice his grimaces and must have them pointed out to him by another archer, who should encourage him by constant correction to let go of these unnecessary tensions.

83. Wrong timing of hanare.

The right moment for hanare comes when physical and mental forces have reached their high point. The release follows the point at which the tension of the draw reaches its peak, resulting in an instant transition of the body to a natural relaxation. Since this is an entirely subjective feeling, it is very difficult for anyone else to tell the archer when the suitable climax in the tension has been reached. Rather he must experience this for himself—which is of course something he can only do after he has made the appropriate efforts.

Being off in one's timing of the release has as a consequence a disturbance in one's feeling of balance during the shot. Either one has released too early or one releases too late, with the result that the bow is overdrawn and shots either go too high or are very weak because the archer has had to let up on the tension in the bow in order to make the release happen at all.

Correction: Since it is difficult for another archer to see and correct this mistake, the archer in question must make an effort on his own to come to the sense of the level of tension that is right for the execution of hanare and feel for himself what the right moment is for the release.

Here let us repeat the reminder that the prerequisite for good hanare is a long and forceful nobiai, which in turn must be based on both physical and mental tension. Such a nobiai must be there for the following hanare to be rightly timed, forceful, and fast.

MISTAKES IN ZANSHIN (84–86)

84. Lack of mental tension in zanshin.

As a rule, this fault is the result of a nobiai and hanare that are weak and deficient in mental tension, with the consequence that, in addition to the faults in shooting technique that result from this, the hanare and the following zanshin appear weak and inelegant.

Correction: The archer must try, especially during nobiai, to stretch the body forcefully and to make his sense of the middle axis of his body increase.

If the occurrence of deficiency in mental tension is caused by temporary illness or particular life circumstances, perhaps the archer should take fewer shots than usual during training sessions, but in the few shots he does take, he should try, despite his altered circumstances, to shoot with all the mental and physical force that is available to him.

Training in kyudo should not be limited exclusively to the physical aspect but, as a fundamental matter, must always also include a proper mental attitude.

85. Loss of balance during hanare.

Mistakes in balance during hanare naturally also have an effect on zanshin. If the archer already commits mistakes (as described above) in structuring his balance during tsumeai, nobiai, and hanare, then these faults in balance must first be corrected before turning to the improvement of zanshin.

Archers should understand that zanshin is exclusively a result of the forces previously at work in nobiai and hanare, and that therefore it is futile and dangerous to try to influence zanshin intentionally or to execute movements after the fact in order to produce the appearance of a correct zanshin. What the archer should do is to try to shape his shooting on the basis of his zanshin—that is, he should seek to execute his draw in such a way that as a result he produces and experiences a proper zanshin.

86. Too long or too short a zanshin.

If an archer has not understood the significance of zanshin, he will do it for too short or too long a time. One has to find the right duration for zanshin by oneself. This proceeds, as we have said, from the proper release of the shot.

Correction: This mistake not only is significant for the individual in question, but also has consequences in competitive shooting, when the archer shoots as part of a group. It can be worked on effectively by paying attention to the breath and using its flow as an indication for the duration of the zanshin. The right timing for zanshin, for taking back the monomi (the gaze to the target), and for yudaoshi (bringing the bow back onto the hip) must always be heeded during normal training and must be correctly executed.

Let us remark in conclusion that zanshin is a criterion for all mistakes made. What has to be done is to learn the basic techniques painstakingly and correctly and always keep up this effort in the course of normal shooting. Of course, this is very difficult. But zanshin will show signs of all the mistakes one has committed.

MISTAKES IN CONCENTRATION (87)

87a. Fear and lack of self-confidence.

These two critical states of mind often appear when competitions are imminent or when the archer's equipment is in bad condition at such times.

In order to avoid having fear come up at all before competitions, one necessity is to be sure to maintain one's equipment so that it does not become a cause for concern; and another is to look at oneself to see what the cause of one's malaise and fears might be.

A clear and open discussion with the teacher or someone who already has experience with shooting in competitions can bring knowledge and insights that might permit the archer to modify his behavior on his own.

87b. Excessive concentration on hitting the target.

When the archer is too willful and concentrates one-sidedly on hitting the bull's eye, his form and the results of his shooting suffer. He becomes cramped, his form becomes inelegant, and he hits the target less often.

Correction: The archer should content himself with the notion that he cannot hit the target any more often than his technique at the moment allows. One-sided expectations and efforts with regard to shot results tend to be counterproductive. Naturally, it is important for an archer to go to a masters tournament with the intention of doing his best. All the same, it is of course not possible to squeeze more out of oneself than is there.

In kyudo, the arrow hits home when we execute the shot correctly. When we think too one-sidedly about hitting the target, our mental attitude changes, and we hit the target less. Therefore, in masters tournaments it is essential not to think about hitting the target but to shoot properly and naturally. Let us repeat here that of course it is important in kyudo to hit the target. However, one can only hit the target when one has learned to repeat the proper technique and the appropriate mental attitude during shooting again and again. Then hitting the target is no longer difficult.

If one does hit the target, one should also take this seriously and not fall into the opposite extreme of becoming cocky and frivolous.

87c. Excessive concentration during shooting.

During shooting it is of course necessary to reflect constantly, to produce a strong intention, and to work on oneself. In working on faults, however, or during competitions, it is a bad thing if, because of one's own opinion or those of other archers, one concentrates one's will excessively on a particular point during shooting. Too much effort often changes the shot for the worse. The archer must try, in accordance with his degree of advancement, to do his best. Nevertheless, he is only capable of taking in and acting upon corrections in accordance with his level of practice and cannot expect suddenly to jump several levels through an extreme application of will.

87d. Arrogance and ambition.

It is not only in kyudo that arrogance, ambition to be the best, and haughtiness toward others represent a deficient mental attitude. Japanese kyudoka have a saying in this connection, *"Tengu wa gei no yukidomari,"* which freely translates as: "Arrogance is the death of the art." The same thing is true of every form of arrogance. The archer must concentrate his entire mental and bodily force on the moment at which he draws his bow and the shot is released. Any accompanying thoughts relating to success, masters honors, or dan degrees can have the result that a part of the archer's available tensile force is spent on these thoughts, and the quality of his shot suffers accordingly.

Exaggerated competitiveness is also ultimately disadvantageous to the archer. He must realize that he can only shoot as well as is permitted by his diligence and the level of practice he has achieved up to this point. It is true that willpower and ambition are necessary in order to practice regularly and at all hard, but it is also essential to be content with whatever results one achieves so that the ability to shoot that the archer has developed up to this point will not be diminished by indulging in unrealistic ideas and desires during shooting.

87e. Mistakes in concentration caused by external circumstances. .

At competitions or examinations, where the audience is more or less known to them, many archers develop heightened ambition in the presence of the these onlookers. Demonstrative or show-off behavior of this sort always results in a lack of proper mental attitude, which becomes evident during the shooting.

Correction: The archer must understand that it is always just himself shooting, no matter what kind of audience is watching him or how large it may be. When an archer comes as part of a team for the first time to a strange dojo, it is often easy for him to develop feelings of not wanting to be conspicuous or make a fool of himself. But regardless of whether the place where he is shooting is unfamiliar and regardless of whether there may be superior archers there, he must attempt to build up his shot just as he is used to doing and to keep himself and the mato at the focal point of his attention while shooting. Similar emotions crop up in all archers when they hear laudatory or critical remarks. The archer must relate to these remarks with equanimity and trust fully in his own skill; and when the time comes, he must prepare and execute his shot through to the end completely independently of these kinds of external hindrances.

For the kyudoka who is already in a position to participate in competitions, it is of absolute importance that, in addition to dealing with the technical problems of shooting, he also be capable of recognizing and working with such psychological problems. Therefore, in the competitive situation, he should not shrink from discussing them with other kyudoka or from openly exchanging insights about how to deal with this kind of phenomenon.

A teacher and trainer of kyudo not only should be knowledgeable about strategies relating to correction of technical faults, but should also be ready with strategies for bringing about a proper state of mind. This can be done both with traditional methods, like those communicated through zazen meditation, and also with Western methods such as discussion or behavior modification.

14

COMPETITION FORMS

For competitions and demonstration shooting, a set of movements is practiced that is connected with the historical tradition of the Heki Ryu. It is used for both standing shooting and kneeling shooting and is essentially identical with the ceremonial-shooting form.

The archers enter the dojo one after the other and place themselves along the honza at the prescribed distances apart, with gaze directed at the target (fig. 14.1). The team bows in the direction of the kamiza and then makes a 90-degree turn to the left to face the mato. The right foot is placed somewhat to the rear, and then all archers kneel on the honza in the *kiza* position—sitting on the heels with the left knee slightly raised (fig. 14.2). The tip of the bow is placed on the ground, and the upper body is inclined forward in a slight bow (*yu*) to the target (fig. 14.3). Then, together, the bows are lifted slightly, and the archers stand.

The archer standing farthest from the kamiza is generally the leader of the team (*ochi*). He now shouts his battle cry (for example, *ku*), and the team repeats the cry right after him. Immediately

FIGURE 14.1

FIGURE 14.2

FIGURE 14.3

FIGURE 14.4

FIGURE 14.5

following the cry, the entire team advances to the shai. This movement is done in three steps, beginning with the left foot, as *matotsuki* (literally, "pushing the target") is being executed (fig. 14.4). In matotsuki, during the forward movement the bow is slowly raised and its tip extended toward the mato. As the last step is completed the right foot is brought up next to the left and the body is turned 90 degrees. The left arm and the bow remain in the matotsuki position. The gaze also remains on the target (fig. 14.5).

The left foot is placed somewhat to the rear, and in this position the archers kneel in such a way that the right knee remains slightly raised from the floor (fig. 14.6). The bow is placed on the hip (fig.

FIGURE 14.6

FIGURE 14.7

FIGURE 14.8

14.7), and after that the gaze is redirected from the mato to the kamiza. The arrows—as a rule, four—are placed by the archer in front of him on the floor. One arrow is picked up and, with the point in the right hand, held on the right hip. Advanced archers can pick up two arrows. In order for the movements of the whole team to be carried out in the most uniform manner possible, in the movements following the advance forward, the archer sitting closest to the kamiza initiates the movements of the sequence. The archers sitting behind him follow him after an appropriate delay.

The front archer now looks at the target, simultaneously lifting his bow, and executes *tekiwari*, or sizing up the target (fig. 14.8).

With a small movement of the left hand, the bowstring is now moved forward, and the bow is set down vertically in front of the body (fig. 14.9).

The right hand is now laid on the right upper thigh in such a way that the archer can look at the arrows in the order of their placement on the string (fig. 14.10).

FIGURE 14.9

FIGURE 14.10

First the haya (first arrow) is nocked, then the otoya (second arrow) is placed beneath the haya between the middle and ring fingers, parallel to the haya but pointing in the opposite direction.

The other archers follow the first archer in these movements one by one. Once the arrows are placed, the right hand is placed on the right hip, and the archer waits in this position until it is his turn to shoot (fig. 14.11). The first archer now takes hold of the string about 25 centimeters below the nocking point and lifts the bow a little off the floor (fig. 14.12). The right knee is placed next to the left on the floor, and then the left knee is raised somewhat

FIGURE 14.11

FIGURE 14.12

FIGURE 14.13

FIGURE 14.14

(fig. 14.13), and from this position the archer stands up. The bow is now held in front of the body, with the arrows approximately at the level of the eyes (fig. 14.14).

Without altering the position of the bow, ashibumi is carried out (figs. 14.15 and 14.16). In dozukuri, the right hand is positioned in front of the middle of the body approximately at the level of the navel (fig. 14.17).

FIGURE 14.15

FIGURE 14.16

FIGURE 14.17

Before yugamae, the bowstring is moved back again to the middle of the body, and the otoya is grasped at the tip by the little and ring fingers of the right hand (fig. 14.18).

The execution of torikake and the remainder of the shot is done in accordance with the basic form (figs. 14.19–14.21).

After zanshin and yudaoshi, the archer redirects his gaze to the kamiza, brings his feet together, and kneels as described earlier.

FIGURE 14.18

FIGURE 14.19

FIGURE 14.20

FIGURE 14.21

After a short pause, he places the next arrow on the string and waits until he can shoot it.

The accepted length of the interval between the individual archers is about the time needed for four stages of the hassetsu; roughly, it means that the archer himself can execute his uchiokoshi when the archer shooting before him has completed his shot.

After the last arrow has been shot, yudaoshi is executed a little bit differently: In the zanshin position, the archer turns his body 90 degrees to the left, makes a half step forward with the right foot, and moves the left foot back next to and parallel to the right foot. During this turn, the left and the right hands are brought back to the hips with a flowing movement.

With the bow tip centered in front of him, the archer now takes three steps backward to the honza, beginning with the right foot; he then kneels down in kiza posture and waits until the entire team has assembled on the honza.

Together then, all the archers again perform a yu to the mato, stand up, take one step backward with the right foot, and leave the dojo.

Variation in the Form for Competitions: In this variation the bow is executed in the standing position. After the team has taken its positions on the honza, the bow tips are placed on the ground. Then, beginning with the first archer, the bow tips are raised 15 centimeters. This lifting of the bows is the signal for the standing bow. After the rei, the sequence of movements runs as described above.

After the last shot, all the archers—with the exception of the team leader at the ochimato—kneel momentarily on the honza. After the ochi has shot his last arrow and has come back to the honza, he remains standing. The other members of the team stand up, and the bow is performed as at the beginning. After the rei, the archers leave the dojo, beginning with a backward step with the right foot.

FORMS OF COMPETITION IN KYUDO

In Japan the competitive life of kyudo is marked by a multitude of matches and masters tournaments.

Competitions are regarded not just as sporting events, but as an essential part of the practice of kyudo, since here the archer can find out if and to what extent his form is already so strong that outer conditions—such as an unfamiliar dojo, the presence of an audience, the tension that goes with eliminations, and team feelings—do not disconcert him in his shooting, leaving him able to shoot with all of his skill.

The following are basic points that govern competitions: The total number of hits on the target decides the victory. If the number of hits is equal, there is a playoff to decide. In team competitions, the team leaders shoot in the playoff; in individual

FIGURE 14.22. *Pan-Japanese Student Masters Tournament in Tokyo, 1976.*

competitions, archers with the same number of points shoot in a playoff; in both cases the playoff continues until a decisive point has been reached. In all competitions, men and women have equal rights.

1. Team Matches
   a. In masters tournaments and similar matches, the team is composed of five archers who each shoot four arrows, making 20 arrows per team.
   b. In league matches, the team is composed of eight archers who each shoot twenty arrows, making a total of 160 arrows per team.
   c. In informal matches, the number of team members (three to eight archers) can vary, and any number of arrows may be decided upon.

2. Individual Matches
   a. In kyudo, team matches predominate, but in these the best individual archers can be indirectly determined. This is done by tallying individual results reached during the match. The winner among archers with the same number of points is determined by a playoff.
   b. To determine the final standing of individuals, four or eight extra arrows are shot. Archers with the same number of points continue to shoot in the playoff match until a decisive result has been reached.
   c. *Izume* (continued hitting the mark) is the name of an individual competition in which archers each shoot one arrow. Any archer who hits the mato has the chance to shoot again; any archer who misses is eliminated. The winner is the last remaining archer. The record for this form of competition still currently rests in the hands of the Waseda Kyudojo, with 22 consecutive hits.

d. Enteki: distance shooting. For women the distances is 50 meters, the standard is 60 meters. The target used is the omato.

e. "Tournament match": individual match in the K.O. system. Competing pairs of archers are chosen by lot. Each archer has two arrows. The winner moves up into the next round, where he shoots against another winner from the previous round. If the result of the final round is a draw, a playoff takes place to decide the victor:

- Each archer shoots two more arrows.
- If this playoff leads to another draw, each archer shoots only one arrow, both at the same target, usually that of the archer in the forward position.
- If the result of this is also a draw, each archer again shoots one arrow at the same target. Now the archer whose shot hits closest to the center of the target is declared the winner.

It is possible in the course of a match for the participants in the last round to be allotted additional playoff chances so as to bring about the fairest possible result. However, such modifications must already have been agreed upon at the beginning of the match.

Masters Tournaments and Matches in Japan

ABBREVIATIONS

NM = normal mato, 36 cm in diameter at a distance of 28 m
IM = individual match
TC = team competition
OM = omato at 60 m distance (enteki); 158 cm in diameter or 79 cm in diameter

1. Pan-Japanese Kyudo Masters (Zen Nihon Zenshiken), NM, IM.
2. Zen Nihon Taikai, NM, IM, with masters tournaments for the titles *hanshi*, *kyoshi*, *renshi*, and *yudansha*, as well as OM shooting.
3. Pan-Japanese Folk Sport Festival, NM, TC, as well as OM, IM. Teams from the prefectures and municipal regions compete with each other according to the K.O. system until there is a winner.
4. Masters tournaments of the prefectures and municipal regions (Tokyo, Kyoto, Osaka), NM, IM, and TC.
5. Masters tournament of the Kyudo Employees group, NM, TC, IM.
6. University and High School Masters Tournament, NM, OM.
7. Pan-Japanese Students Kyudo Masters Tournament, NM, TC, and IM.
8. High School Teachers Kyudo Masters Tournament, NM.
9. Student intraregional masters tournaments (six regions), NM, TC, and IM.
10. League competitions of the kyudojo in seven skill levels, NM, TC, and IM.
11. Individual matches between the best league archers, NM.
12. East-West Students Masters Tournament, NM, TC, and IM.
13. High school masters tournaments in the prefectures and municipal regions, as well as pan-Japanese high school masters tournaments, NM, TC, and IM.
14. O.B. masters tournament (masters tournament of former students), NM, TC, and IM.
15. Tenran (shooting in front of the imperial court) by the best archers of the prefectures, NM, IM.
16. Competition of the best teams of the Heki, Honda, and Ogasawara Ryu against one another.

弓
道

15

EXAMINATION FORMS

IN KYU AND DAN examinations, shots are executed in front of the examination committee in a special, established way. Each examinee shoots two arrows according to a movements scheme that is the same for all kyudoka, regardless of what school they come from. This standard form of the Zen Nihon Kyudo Renmei, Pan-Japanese Kyudo Society, is shown in the illustrations as performed by a single archer. In the real examination, this movements form is executed in a group.

The examinees, usually five, enter the dojo one after the other with bow and arrow. The arrows are held by the tip in the right hand at the level of the hip. The tip of the bow is about 15 centimeters off the floor, centered in front of the archer. In this position, which resembles the basic position, the archers walk to their appropriate places on the honza. There they make a 90-degree standing turn, so that they end up with their gaze directed toward the mato, then assume the kiza posture (sitting on the heels with the left knee slightly raised) on the honza (fig. 15.1). A yu to the mato is executed (figs. 15.2 and 15.3). After this, the archers stand

FIGURE 15.1

FIGURE 15.2

FIGURE 15.3

FIGURE 15.4

FIGURE 15.5

FIGURE 15.6

and walk forward to the shooting position (shai) in three steps, beginning with the left foot.

If there is already a group of examinees shooting, the following examinees stand up on the honza at the sound made by the second to the last of the preceding archers as he releases his shot. Then they wait until the last of the preceding archers has moved his bow back to the hip after shooting, and at this moment begin their advance to the shooting position.

- The archers kneel on the shai with the right foot positioned slightly back and their gaze directed toward the mato (fig. 15.4).
- The right knee is moved next to the left so that both knees are touching the floor. The toes remain curved forward (fig. 15.5).
- The pelvis and trunk are raised, and at the same time the upper tip of the bow is brought up approximately to the level of the eyes (fig. 15.6).

FIGURE 15.7

FIGURE 15.8

FIGURE 15.9

FIGURE 15.10 · FIGURE 15.11

- The left lower thigh is turned out 90 degrees to the left without the knee leaving the floor (fig. 15.7, front view; fig. 15.8, rear view).
- The right leg and the body are turned rearward so that the archer now looks toward the front side of the kyudojo (*wakishomen* or *kamiza*).
- The bow is moved to a vertical position in front of the middle of the body (fig. 15.9), and the left knee is slightly lifted.
- The bow is grasped by the string below the level of the grip and turned (figs. 15.10 and 15.11).

The arrows are placed:

- First the haya is nocked on the string.
- Then the otoya is placed, pointing backward, beneath the haya and parallel to it, between the middle and ring fingers.

- The right hand is placed on the right hip until it is time to stand up (fig. 15.12).

Standing up:

- The right hand grasps the string at the nocking point with all fingers extended (fig. 15.13). (The original form, also customary in competitions, is that the bowstring is held about 30 centimeters below the arrow.)
- The archer stands, using the left leg. The bow remains vertical, and the hands hold the bow in such a way that the arrows are at eye level (fig. 15.14).

Execution of ashibumi:

- This is done as usual, with the exception that the gaze is directed toward the target over the arrow.

Execution of dozukuri:

- The string remains in front of the middle of the body, the right hand is placed on the right hip sideways (fig. 15.15), and *tsurushirabe* (checking of the string) is executed.
- The gaze moves calmly and evenly from the nocking point upward to the end of the string, then downward to the other end of the bow and back to the nocking point (fig. 15.16).
- Starting with the nock, the gaze moves along the arrow to the mato and back again. In doing this, the head should not be conspicuously moved but should remain as still as possible (fig. 15.17). The tsurushirabe is not done in the competition form, only in the examination form.

FIGURE 15.12

FIGURE 15.13

FIGURE 15.14

FIGURE 15.15

FIGURE 15.16

FIGURE 15.17

FIGURE 15.18

Execution of hassetsu (fig. 15.18), zanshin, and yudaoshi (moving the bow back to the hip):

- Kneel again as above.

  Before continuing, the first archer waits, kneeling, with bow raised and arrow placed, for the sound the last archer (shooting his first shot) makes at the release of his shot. After hearing the sound, he stands up and shoots his second arrow.

For the time interval between the remaining archers, this is the rule:

- At the sound of the release of the archer currently shooting, the following archer should execute uchiokoshi. His preparation must be completed by this time.

  When the second arrow has been shot, the archer takes the bow back onto his hip, turns his head again in the direction of the wakishomen (the right side of the dojo), comes out of his ashibumi, puts his feet back together, and takes three steps on the diagonal forward and to the right so that the examiners can have a full view of the next archer. After these three steps, the archer turns toward the honza, lifts his bow vertically, and leaves the dojo, walking behind the archers sitting on the honza. The last archer also takes his bow back onto his hip, but instead of walking forward takes two steps back and then makes a right-angle turn in the direction of the dojo exit.

RULES FOR EXAMINATIONS

General Regulations

The examination rules have the purpose of awarding kyudo practitioners a kyu or dan degree that corresponds to their achievement in kyudo and their attitude toward the practice. In this way, kyudo can be promoted while maintaining its standards.

The kyu degrees go from 5 to 1, the dan degrees in ten stages from 1 to 10. Certificates are issued for the kyu and dan degrees; colored symbols such as belts do not exist.

Two examinations must be separated by a minimum preparatory period of six months; however, in cases of extraordinary achievement, one degree (at the most) can be skipped if it is proved by an examination that the candidate can perform at the required level.

The examinations are composed of a practical and a theoretical part. From the first kyu on, the theoretical part takes the form of a written test (a questionnaire or a treatment of a kyudo theme in which evaluative positions are taken).

For the practical examination, two shots are required following the *taihai* method (set of movements) of the ANKF (called here "Examinations Forms"), which the examinations committee judges.*

The examination is considered to have been passed when the conditions indicated in figure 15.19 have been met.

Examination Qualifications for Kyudo Kyu Degrees

5TH KYU
- Dojo etiquette.
- Handling of equipment that is necessary for shooting (care of bows, gloves, and arrows; correct stringing and unstringing of the bow; care and reinforcement of bowstrings with correct tsuruwa and nakashikake).

* Information about the taihai in this chapter stems from the 1970s, when this text was first written; several changes have since taken place. The English version of the ANKF Kyudo Manual shows the actual standard.

–EDITOR

DEGREE SOUGHT	NUMBER AND DEGREE LEVEL OF EXAMINERS	REQUIRED PERCENTAGE OR NUMBER OF APPROVING EXAMINERS
5TH TO 1ST KYU	2 OF 3RD DAN AND ABOVE	2
1ST TO 4TH DAN	3 RENSHI AND/OR KYOSHI	2
	5 RENSHI AND/OR KYOSHI	3
5TH DAN	5 OR MORE KYOSHI AND/OR HANSHI	70%
6TH DAN	5 OR MORE KYOSHI AND/OR HANSHI	70%
7TH DAN AND HIGHER	7 HANSHI (KYOSHI)	80%

FIGURE 15.19. *Conditions for passing examinations.*

- The hassetsu sequence has been correctly learned, and the form is by and large in order.
- All stages of shooting are to be executed with an arrow in place in front of the makiwara.

4TH KYU

- All skills of the 5th kyu must be mastered.
- Handling of equipment has progressed to the point where the candidate is capable of carrying out all usual work on the equipment by himself: shortening and reinforcing of strings, wrapping the leather grip, insertion of arrow nocks, points, and feathers. The basic points of the construction and character of the Japanese bow must be familiar. Knowledge of the various target configurations and of how to make a mato must be demonstrated.
- The hassetsu sequence is executed smoothly. Form of shooting an arrow has been well enough learned in front of the makiwara that it is now possible to shoot at the mato.

3RD KYU

- All the skills of the preceding examination levels must be mastered.
- The general movements of shooting (hassetsu) have been learned, and the handling of the bow and arrow has been understood. It should be determined whether the practitioner is receiving appropriate instruction. This includes the movements before and after shooting (*dosa*). The examination takes place in front of the mato.

2ND KYU

Execution and performance level of shooting shows progress over the 3rd kyu. The release of the shot (hanare) takes place smoothly (continuous extension of nobiai).

1ST KYU

It should be determined that the shooting form and the movements before and after shooting are by and large correct. The movements are carried out with attention and care. Shots go in the direction of the mato.

Examination Qualifications for Kyudo Dan Degrees

1ST (SHO) DAN

The shooting form and the movements before and after shooting correspond to the standard form. Arrows shot concentrate in the vicinity of the target with a maximum divergence of 45 centimeters.

2ND (NI) DAN

Shooting form and movements are in the right order and correspond to the standard form. The relationship of forces in the draw is right. Shots show a circumscribed, just slight scattering, and at least one arrow must hit the target.

3RD (SAN) DAN

The shooting form is established, the movements before and after shooting have become natural, breathing is right, and movements are coordinated with it. The technique is in harmony with the basic form, arrows fly straight, and 50 percent of them hit the target.

4TH (YON) DAN

The level of the 3rd dan has been mastered. The hanare is forceful and sharp. The target must be hit (that is, in the examination both arrows have to hit the target).

5TH (GO) DAN

Shooting form, technique, and movements are in accordance with the rules. Refinement and elegance can be expressed with the bow. The various aspects of kyudo have been well studied. The target must be hit.

The aspects of kyudo are set down in the *Rokka*, or "Six Subjects": *kyuri* (theory of the technique), *kyurei* (ceremony and form), *kyuho* (handling of equipment), *kyuko* (fabrication), *kyuki* (equipment), and *renshin* (training the mind).

6TH (ROKU) DAN

It should be determined that the technique has developed to the point of excellence. The aspects of kyudo have been very well studied, and refinement of mind and knowledge are expressed.

7TH (SHICHI) DAN

Form, technique, and movement arise of themselves. A high degree of refinement has been reached, and the level of an expert has been reached.

8TH (HACHI) DAN

The technical abilities have become mature, refined, and

elegant. Artfulness has reached the point of excellence and is masterfully integrated with the technique.

Note: Creative force, character, and the archer's own sense of kyudo are included in the presentation of the art and technique.

9TH (KU) DAN

The essence of kyudo is transparently visible in the person.

10TH (JU) DAN

The art has been become transparent in the person.

Rules for Conferring Titles

In addition to the degrees, titles can also be conferred on members of the kyudo organization who have made noteworthy achievements through study and practice.

Honorary titles are renshi, kyoshi, and hanshi.

The kyudo dan degrees of the Heki Ryu also have a six-level system of titles (see the section "Examination Qualifications for Kyudo Dan Degrees").

The titles renshi and kyoshi and the Heki titles are conferred on the basis of an examination. The title hanshi is conferred on the basis of a nomination. All the titles require a minimum of previously earned degrees. This is described in more detail below.

The titles have the following meanings:

- *Hanshi* is, in person and in art and technique, an example for others.
- *Kyoshi* has shown in the course of training and practice good and very good abilities in teaching.
- *Renshi* has shown in the course of training and practice a good level of experience in teaching.

Candidates have to fulfill the following requirements:

Examination Subjects	Kyu Degree					Dan Degree				
	5	4	3	2	1	1	2	3	4	5
1. Haya hits / Otoya hits			X	X	X	X	X	X	X	X
2. Ashibumi / Dozukuri / Yugamae	X	X	X	X	X	X	X	X	X	X
3. Uchiokoshi / Sambun no ni / Tsumeai	X	X	X	X	X	X	X	X	X	X
4. Nobiai	X	X	X	X	X	X	X	X	X	X
5. Hanare	X	X	X	X	X	X	X	X	X	X
6. Zanshin	X	X	X	X	X	X	X	X	X	X
7. Taihai (set of movements)			X	X	X	X	X	X	X	X
8. Dojo etiquette	X	X	X	X	X	X				
9. Skills			X	X	X				X	
10. Theory					X	X	X	X	X	X
11. Ability to teach							X	X	X	X
12. Association course participation (at least 20 classes in the examination year)				X	X	X	X	X	X	X

FIGURE 15.20. *Examination subjects for kyudo dan degrees.*

- *Hanshi:* Holder of the 8th dan degree. He must embody virtue and purity, mature skill, and a high level of knowledge. Especially, he must be an outstanding example in the world of kyudo.
- *Kyoshi:* Holder of the 6th dan degree and a renshi. He must possess character, skill, and wisdom. He must have attained the culture necessary for teaching kyudo as well as noteworthy knowledge and ability in archery.

- *Renshi:* Holder of the 5th dan degree. He must possess stability (principles and steadiness) as well as the ability to teach. His skill must be polished, and he must have achieved noteworthy results.

There is a committee in the kyudo organization that oversees proper assessment in conferring these titles.

In particularly justified exceptional cases, it is possible for someone to be selected for one of these titles without these requirements having been fulfilled. It is also possible to confer a title posthumously in a case where it was not possible to grant it during the lifetime of a noteworthy person who did possess these qualifications. But both these types of cases are exceptions, and such matters must be handled strictly and fairly.

If the holder of a title violates or damages the honor of the title, or if he behaves in a fashion contrary to the rules of the organization, the title must be renounced, or it may be revoked and declared invalid.

Titles of the Heki Ryu

Jun mokuroku (Quasi-mokuroku). This title corresponds to at least the 2nd or 3rd dan. Every aspect of Heki Ryu archery has been learned and has on the whole developed to a mature level. The methods of the Heki Ryu, the kan chu kyu (speed; penetrating force; endurance, continuity), have been understood, and it is certain that in the future the methods of the Heki Ryu will be perpetuated.

Mokuroku (The "Table of Contents" Scroll). This title corresponds to at least the 4th to 5th dan. The candidate must possess more than the 4th dan according to the Pan-Japanese Kyudo Society degree system, and more than three years must have passed since receipt of the jun mokuroku. It must be recognized that progress in the practice and the art has taken place, that the heart is upright, that in daily life the recipient is an example for others and that he will preserve the honor of the Heki Ryu.

Mugonka (The "Song without Words" Scroll). This title corresponds to at least the 6th to 7th dan. The recipient surpasses others in his training deportment and in his practice attitude. Character, art, and knowledge are all outstanding. He has the ability to teach younger people.

Shindo (Shinto) no maki (The "Way of the Gods" Scroll). This title corresponds to at least the 8th dan and is conferred on the basis of nomination, and then only after painstaking critical analysis and consideration on the part of the organization.

Shinanhyakushu (The "Hundred Songs of Instruction" Scroll). This title corresponds to at least the 9th dan.

16

TARGET GAMES:
Matoasobi

On special occasions, as at the end of a training camp or competition, or else on the occasion of the New Year, *matoasobi* are arranged by the kyudoka. These target games are a light-hearted version of archery, which should above all be fun for the participants. The matoasobi are usually started off with four shots at the normal hoshimato and concluded with shooting at the gold and silver targets. In between, the various different types of targets can be used for the games in any sequence and according to any system of scoring.

Kohaku: White and Red

The mato here consists of a circle of 45 centimeters in diameter that is divided vertically into white and red half-circles. Shooting happens in two rounds of two arrows each, with the red half on the left for one round and on the right for the other. Two archers shoot simultaneously at this mato, but with the proviso that the archer in the front position can only shoot at the rear field of the mato and the archer in the back position can only shoot at the front field of the mato.

If the mato is missed, no points are given. If the wrong field is hit, then there are minus points. A hit on the appropriate part of the target is rewarded with a high number of points.

Shichigosan: 7-5-3

In this contest, a normal mato of 36 centimeters is used, the front side of which is divided through the use of various colors into three rings of the same size. The rings are marked with appropriate numbers for scoring hits: the inner ring 7 points, the middle ring 5, and the outer ring 3. Ordinarily, four arrows are shot at this target.

Sandanmato

"Three-step mato" is the literal translation of *sandanmato*, since three different sizes of target disks are used (15, 24, and 36 cm). Here, too, with this configuration of targets, shooting is in teams of two. Each archer begins with three arrows. First an arrow is shot at the big mato. If it hits, the next archer shoots at the next smallest, and so on. Any method of scoring can be used. If all three mats are hit in the first round, this round is over. If all three mato are hit only after the third or fourth round, the hits score less in each succeeding round.

Iwarimato

Iwari literally means, "to split something by shooting." And here in fact a square panel of wood is split that is from 15 to 20 centimeters on a side and is set up point upward on a stick at a distance of 20 to 24 meters from the archers. The midpoint of the panel must be at the height normal for the flight path of an arrow being shot at a target set at 28 meters. On the back side of this panel of light, easily breakable wood, a small paper bag filled with confetti is placed. If the iwarimato is hit, the bag breaks, and a colorful cloud of confetti flies in all directions.

Each archer shooting at the iwarimato is normally allowed two arrows.

Omato

For the big mato, the colored targets used for Olympic archery serve very well. The different rings are assigned appropriate point values. Each archer shoots two arrows at the Omato.

Tateichi-Yokoichi

This target game gets its name from the way the "one" is written in Japanese, which is *ichi;* and the number sign is drawn once as a vertical stroke (*tate*) and then once as a horizontal stroke (*yoko*). The "one" at which one shoots here consists of a surface of 60 by 15 centimeters, with a black circle of 10 centimeters in the middle. One of these is set up vertically and another on its side in the target area. Each archer gets two arrows for each position.

Oginomato

Oginomato means "fan target." A simple paper fan is either hung on a string from the roof beam of the target area in front of the azuchi or set up like an iwarimato on a stick in the area in front of it. Each archer shoots two arrows at this target.

The style of this target goes back to a famous incident in the Heike wars against the Genji. In the battle of Dannoura, the Minamoto conclusively defeated the Taira family, thus ending the Gempei war in its favor. The initial situation in this decisive battle was as follows. The Taira family had withdrawn with its fleet onto the sea, while the Minamoto family, under the command of

FIGURE 16.1. *The samurai Naso no Yoichi riding through the sea (woodcut).*

General Yoshitsune Minamoto, was on the shore. The story goes that in this battle, near Yashima, a small boat, on whose mast a lady of the court had hung up her fan, separated itself from the mass of war junks. At this, Minamoto Yoshitsune commanded one of his samurai to shoot down the fan. The samurai Naso no Yoichi, who was only seventeen years old, leaped onto his horse, rode into the sea, and shot at this target that was fixed to the rocking mast and blowing in the wind at the same time (fig. 16.1). But his art, his skill, was so great that he struck the fan exactly at the point where its struts came together, so that it not only came loose from its fastenings but also burst into its component parts. An immense cheer rose from the Minamoto side at this masterful shot. The shot may not—as legend recounts— have decided the battle, but its psychological effect, during a period when much store was set on auspicious signs, should not be underestimated.

Kinteki and Ginteki (Gold and Silver Targets)

A wooden or cardboard hoop with a diameter of 10 to 12 centimeters is covered with gold or silver paper. One gold and one silver mato are set up in the target area with their midpoints at the same height as that of a normal mato and in such a way that the light can reflect well off the gold and silver surfaces. Then in addition, at a diameter corresponding to that of a normal mato, green branches are laid around these brilliant centers. Each archer gets one shot at the gold and one at the silver mato. However, once a mato has been hit by a fortunate archer, then only one of these mato, which have been described as bringers of good fortune, remains available. This target game ends when both of the matos have been struck.

Star Sign

A favorite thing to do for the New Year is to shoot at a normal mato that has an animal painted on it, representing that year according to the Chinese zodiac: rat, ox, tiger, hare, dragon, snake, horse, goat, monkey, cock, dog, and boar. For the archer who succeeds in hitting the eye of the animal, it is supposed to be a lucky year.

Since in the matoasobi the scoring system (minus points, varying big scores for hits or misses) is arbitrarily set by the participants, the final results, when all the shots are added up, can sometimes be quite surprising.

In Japan, frequently every participant contributes a small gift, which he leaves with the dojo head before the competition. The dojo head then distributes these after the competition. In this way, no one goes home empty-handed, and everyone has fun.

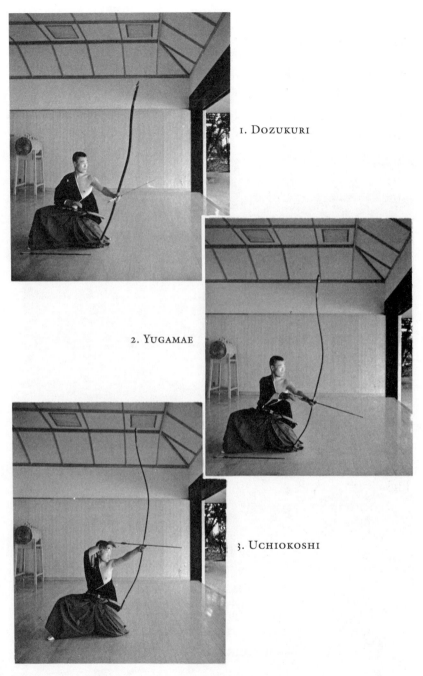

1. DOZUKURI

2. YUGAMAE

3. UCHIOKOSHI

FIGURE 16.2. *Inagaki Sensei performing warihiza (ceremonial shooting in kneeling position) in the dojo of the Meiji Jingu (Meiji Shrine Park) in Tokyo.*

4. Sanbun no ni

5. Nobiai

6. Zanshin

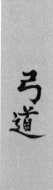

17

SPECIAL FORMS OF SHOOTING

Sharei: Ceremonial Shooting

As early as the sixth century, ceremonial archery took place at the imperial court. This was called *jarai*, and it later developed into an official ceremony for the beginning of the New Year. From the eighth to eleventh centuries, this New Year's ceremony was reserved for the members of the imperial court, but since approximately the thirteenth century, during the rule of the shogunate, this event was enacted by many samurai and was called *onmato hajime*. The ceremonial shooting of today, sharei, contains the essential features of these historic forms of shooting.

The ceremonies can be presented in the form of either individual or group shooting. In the Mochimato ceremony, each archer shoots at his own target, whereas in the ceremonial form known as Hitotsumato, three archers, one after the other, shoot at one target. The ceremony is always performed in a kimono. Along with the ceremonial forms that are followed by all schools and are supported by the Zen Nihon Kyudo Renmei, the individual schools have also preserved their own original forms of the ceremonies and continue to practice them today. There are two basic forms of the ceremony, one that takes place in a dojo in which the archers can kneel, and a ceremonial form that is performed outdoors, meaning that the archer bows and shoots only while standing.

In the Heki Ryu, in a full ceremony two arrows are shot standing and two are shot kneeling. At all ceremonies, an assistant is present who can aid the archer in case complications arise while he is removing his arm from the wide sleeve of the kimono, in case the bowstring should break, or in case the glove comes loose. The assistant stands by to help in those circumstances. He also retrieves from the target area the arrows shot by the archer and returns them to the archer. His place is behind and somewhat to the right of the archer, and he bows whenever the archer does.

The ceremony will not be described in further detail here. It basically corresponds to the form used for competitions. At the beginning, in addition to the greeting bow to the mato, a deep bow is also made to the kamiza, and the removing and putting back on of the kimono sleeve are done in accordance with a precise, fixed scheme of movements.

In shooting from the kneeling position, a particularity worth mentioning is that the second arrow is not held in the right hand after dozukuri, but is placed on the floor in front of the archer. Study of the ceremonial forms becomes interesting and possible for students from the 4th dan on (see photo #5 in fig. 16.2).

Enteki

The term *enteki* refers to shooting at the long-distance target, in which men have to shoot a distance of 60 meters and women a distance of 50 meters. The target used is a mato of 158 centimeters in diameter (omato), which is stretched on a wooden frame. But there is also enteki shooting in which a target only 79 centimeters in diameter (*hanmato*) is used.

Kazuya and Koshiya

Kazuya and koshiya are historical shooting methods used in war. The form that has been handed down to the present day is essentially derived from the infantry tactics of the Satsuma clan from Kagoshima Prefecture. The archer carries, in addition to his bow, other historical weapons and pieces of equipment, such as armor, a naked sword, a hip quiver (ebira), leg protectors, sandals, a typical thumb-shaped cap (*boshi*), or even a large helmet (*kabuto*), and a frightening face mask (*menpo*). In contrast to the way kyudo is practiced now, in kazuya and koshiya, shots are released with a *kiai*, a battle shout.

Proceedings begin with the kazuya. The archer squats on both heels with the left knee propped against the ground and a bunch of arrows lying against the right upper thigh. At this point the object is to shoot a great number of arrows into the target one after the other as quickly as possible. Kazuya is a method of "fast shooting" (*kazu* = number, *ya* = arrow) that was particularly used against an enemy that was quite far away, for example, advancing cavalry. Once the enemy had moved close enough, the form of shooting was changed, and koshiya—fast but aimed shooting—began. Without taking his eyes off the enemy, the archer drew an arrow out of the hip quiver, placed it on the string, and shot it off, then nocked another arrow and ran toward the enemy with his arrow in place; then stopped running and knelt again, shot, took another arrow from the quiver, and so on. Having come to within a few meters of the target, he then took his bow under his arm and used it as a thrusting weapon, accompanying his thrust with a long kiai. It was not at all unusual to use the bow as a thrusting weapon. Often war bows had a lance set into the tip, or else—if his string had broken—the archer bound his short sword onto the upper end of his bow and then used it as a *naginata* (sword spear).

In koshiya and kazuya, gloves are used that come closer to the historical model than the yugake that is common today. They usually have a relatively soft thumb. The arrows, too, are made to resemble historical models. They have an end shaped like a swallow's tail and a sharp point. The fast nocking, the different kind of glove,

FIGURE 17.1. *Kazuya.*

FIGURE 17.2. *Koshiya.*

FIGURE 17.3. *Koshiyakiyumi kagoshima archers performing group shooting at the 1964 Olympics.*

and wearing a helmet all make another manner of drawing and re-leasing necessary. Therefore, kazuya and koshiya have to be learned on their own as forms of shooting, and thus they remain reserved for advanced archers (figs. 17.1–17.3).

Hikime

Since prehistoric times, the Japanese have believed that with the help of a bow and arrow it is possible to exorcise all manner of evil as well as to bring about peace and happiness. Two ceremonies, meigen and *hikime*, have been handed down from mythological times (fig. 17.4)

In the hikime ceremony, a special arrow with a flute for a tip—*hikimeya*—is shot. The sound of this arrow brings good fortune and purifies the atmosphere through which it has flown. In this way all evil spirits are driven away. For these reasons, a hikime arrow is shot over a house at the birth of a child. In this case, the ceremony is called *tanjohikime*. If a flute arrow is shot over the house of a sick person, this is called *yagoshihikime*. These two ceremonies are executed only by archers of a very high dan level. The ceremonies require special preparation—for example, purification before shooting—as well as a special costume, which resembles the garb of a Shinto

FIGURE 17.4. *Meigen ceremony, Master Urakami Sake, 10th dan hanshi. (Photo: Waseda Dojo)*

priest. All this is considered necessary if the desired effect of the flute arrow is to be achieved.

Yabusame

A very well known yet quite extraordinary form of shooting is yabusame, archery on horseback, which came to flourish in the twelfth century through an imperial decree. In the thirteenth century, this form of shooting was fostered in particular by the shogun Minamoto Yoritomo. Competitions in yabusame take place to the present day, in September at the Hachiman Shrine (Hachiman is a Shinto war god) in Kamakura.

In the competitions, the archers wear a hunting costume from the Kamakura period (fig. 17.5). They must ride without the use of their hands at a full gallop along the 256–meter yabusame track. As they ride by, the archers must hit three targets, which are similar to the iwarimato (a rhombus, approximately 30 centimeters on a side), in such a way that the target bursts. The targets are placed about 2 meters above the ground and about 3 meters from the riding path. Measured from the starting point, the targets are at 37, 115, and 188 meters (fig. 17.6). The yabusame style is taught in the Takeda and Ogasawara schools. Because of the special materials and its space requirements, yabusame is reserved for the very few.

FIGURE 17.5. *Yabusame master Kaneko Yurin.*

FIGURE 17.6.
Yabusame.

Toshiya

The toshiya form of shooting was done on the west veranda of the famous Sanjusangendo Temple for the first time in 1609. The requirements of the competition were such that each archer shot for twenty-four hours without interruption, trying to get as many arrows as possible into the target at the north end of the temple from the shooting point at the south end of the temple. Along with the great distance, the principal difficulty for the archer is that the flight path of his arrows is bounded on the right by the thirty-three niches (sanjusangendo), the deck of the veranda, and

FIGURE 17.7. Toshiya, *woodcut by Utagawa Tokoyane.*

the rafters of the roof. The competition began each evening at six o'clock, and after each five hundred arrows, which the archer had to get to fly the 118-meter distance to the target, a short break was taken. The record was held for a long time by a samurai named Hoshino, who shot 10,542 arrows, of which 8,000 reached the target. He was beaten in 1686 by Wasa Daihachiro, who was only twenty-two. Wasa's record, which remains unbeaten today, was a total of 13,053 arrows, with 8133 hitting the target. This corresponds to an average shooting speed of ten arrows per minute.

Each year on "Coming of Age Day" in January, a large toshiya event takes place on the temple grounds alongside the veranda where the original toshiya competition took place (fig. 17.7).

弓道

18

YUMI NO KOKORO:*
THE MIND BORN OF
ARCHERY

— GENSHIRO INAGAKI

NORMALLY THE REASONS for kyudo, the goals one would like to achieve through it, are not defined. Many pursue kyudo as a hobby or just a sport.

But in Japan, there are also other groups that would like to associate kyudo, as one of the kinds of budo, with a particular way of life. One of these groups learns kyudo as a particular kind of ceremony. They believe that when, through practice, the ceremony gets better, that is progress in the art of archery. But this is an illusion.

The art of archery lies in harvesting the fruits that grow from one's skill in archery and from one's mind. Kyudo includes both: skill and mind. That gets forgotten. For this reason, the following

* This chapter is an English translation of a translation from German by Professor Manfred Speidel, who also edited the text.

is true: Whoever practices properly with the bow will also make progress in the mind. Only through practicing the technique, or art, of archery does it become possible to enter upon the Way of the Bow. Whoever neglects the difficult technique, whoever thinks he can travel this Way by means of the ceremony, remains stuck with the mere form. Of course, the ceremony also has its value, but that is the world of ceremony, not the world of the Bow.

Another group says: Kyudo is the way of the mind. Its goal is to cultivate the mind. In the opinion of this group, the mind is the most important and highest thing. In this kyudo of the mind, the art of the bow, the technique, is a fringe problem. But here too there is faulty thinking.

Of course, to some extent both groups reach their goal.

Those who practice archery as a ceremony, who refine their form, polish their movements so that they become beautiful and give an impression of elegance—they too attain to a heart moved by the mind; they too may penetrate to a certain degree into the phase of non-ego.

And those who seek the kyudo of the mind, who draw the bow and linger at the moment of the full draw, they too can enter into the state of non-ego in this way—I know this from my own experience.

However, this static state of non-ego reached by means of a particular position and movement of the body dissipates in most cases when the form changes. One returns without delay into the world of ego.

Multifold repetition of this form, the effort of concentrating the mind and stabilizing the emotions, surely have a good influence on everyday life. The normal person might think that these fruits are already the goal that was to be attained, and there is not much to oppose to this opinion.

However, the goal of our practice in archery is, by means of these (spiritual) exercises, to attain clarity stage by stage. Clarity about the nature of the human mind—to recognize and see with precision, to experience physically that there is an origin of one's own mind, that the mind does not think anything and also has no thoughts, but that it nevertheless can see and judge everything precisely. To have things before one's eyes and see, to clearly recognize their nature. With an "Oh, so it is like that?" "Is that so?" "Was it like that?" it comes off one's lips, it is discovered, the mind is discovered in a physical way. That is the goal of archery. One discovers, knows, sees that only when one practices kyudo.

The Zen master Koun Suhara of Engaku Temple—my kyudo friend whom, however, from the point of view of his mental attitude I regard as my older brother—said to me that he wanted to practice kyudo to attain this goal that I have described, in order to experience the Mind of the Bow for himself.

I do not say that Zen and archery necessarily have to go together. I am not going to say so. It is true one might suspect that Zen and kyudo are the same; but if one does not come to this conclusion, that's okay too. I think one may come very close to Zen, but in my opinion one shouldn't ingratiate oneself with Zen, try to get in good with Zen. Zen and kyudo attain the same degree of enlightenment. And we have the certainty that the mind is developed and educated just as much by kyudo as by Zen.

On the basis of my own experience, I would like to speak to you about the relationship between technique and mind. My words are taken from the everyday experience of kyudo and are not so much a matter of science. I am nevertheless convinced that they do not contain any mistakes.

The achievement of mind comes about, people say, through a conditioned reflex. The conditioned reflex is the cause. But beyond this, there is another idea of what the mind is.

Based on my forty-seven years of shooting the bow, I espouse a two-origins theory.

In Japan, as a general rule, the beginner practices every day, and in so doing executes about one hundred shots a day. After two to three years, a number of archers reach an elevated proportion of hits on the target. During this period of time, the instructions of the teacher have been faithfully followed; the archer has worked one-pointedly, attentively, and hard.

In any case, the repetition and the undisturbed, continuous process have made the movements of the archer into conditioned reflexes. The skill will then one day bring forth its fruits, and the archer will at some time achieve an astonishingly high number of precise hits, frequently better results than someone who has practiced for a longer time.

However, one day he will direct his attention to the release of the shot (hanare). This time will come for sure. His hanare is not yet the hanare that arises when a shot is consciously and perfectly built up from the ashibumi through all the stages. That means the following: When he makes his shot on the basis of conditioned reflexes, he hits the target, if this state is good (that is, if he is well conditioned). Such an archer normally appears quite advanced— of course, only if one has only known him for a short time. By comparison with a better archer, one makes out weaknesses in his skill. If the reflexes he has developed have made it possible for the archer to become good, he no longer has to pay attention to his skill. His mind, his heart, is suddenly set free. If he continues to shoot in such a state, his awakening, deepening, and broadening mind will discover what is lacking in his own technique, what the weak points are. If he then wants to improve, an insuppressible impulse bursts forth. He suddenly feels uncertain in his current state and enters a state that is no longer one of non-ego. At this point his pattern of reflexes falls apart. He can suddenly no longer shoot the way he did before. At the moment of kai—the full draw—disturbing thoughts and wild fantasies intervene. The mind is moved here and there by questions; the hanare becomes faulty. But the true training in kyudo begins here.

Is the present state of the technique good? Is the skill correct? What should one do to improve? One's own practiced form, from ashibumi to zanshin, becomes dependent on the present state, the desire (or lack of desire) of the heart; countless doubts, one's mind tossing about here and there, thoughts cropping up that become soundless words, which in turn produce other thoughts, which then develop further and cast his technique into chaos. Here is an important point. This confusion of the heart can be avoided if one begins shooting afresh starting from the mato, if one lets kyudo develop again out of the skill.

Those who advocate the kyudo of the mind would then say: Forget the mato, put it out of your mind. (Such teachers have existed and still exist.) But this is a prejudice regarding technique, and technique leads these people around by the nose. Therefore they fear it and reject it. Perhaps one can overcome this crisis for a period of time if one forgets the technique or puts it totally aside, and one comes perhaps into the realm of non-ego. But those who would propagate the kyudo of the mind make a big mistake here.

The original goal of this group was—was it not?—to achieve the kyudo of the mind by means of archery. If they now forget that they have chosen the art of archery (the nerve center of which is precisely the skill or technique of it), then they deny archery. That one reaches a certain level through Zen is affirmed by everyone. Even if only an external form is imitated, I can still agree that there is a parallel to the way of Zen. The conditions are the same: breathing and a specific form of tension and concentration. But that is then a kind of Zen that has borrowed the Form of the Bow, in which the Bow is employed as a means. But that is not kyudo.

A Zen master well known in Japan said that kyudo was a part of Zen, was a means of grasping Zen. Whether this statement is true or false, I don't know, but he is an outsider as far as kyudo is concerned. He is of the opinion that Zen is almighty and self-sufficient.

Kyudo is mind and skill, a union of both. Depending on how perfect one's art is, or how close to perfection it comes, spiritual fruits are plucked, and these fruits will help us to attain a higher level as human beings and to attain spiritual wealth. It is true that this goes in the same direction as Zen, but it is not Zen, it is kyudo. Various fruits of supreme well-being and bliss that can be acquired through kyudo cannot be acquired through Zen.

What, then, is actually the mind that can be achieved through archery, the mind awakened by the Bow? How do we come to it, or how does the archer realize this mind as his own? What kind of a thing is it? What is it that is so special that one acquires when one pursues the art to its limits, penetrates the technique to the ultimate point?

The sword fighter Miyamoto Musashi, who was born in the seventeenth century and was unsurpassed in Japan, presented the secret principles of sword fighting in his book *Go Rin No Sho*, "The Five Important Factors (of the Body)." In the last chapter of the scroll, *Ku no maki*, "The Role of Nothingness," he said about technique: "He who reaches the high point of the art no longer has any doubt and fear himself; when he confronts an enemy, he does nothing and also thinks nothing; he moves as his awakened heart shows him. This state is the state of eternal peace, without enemies."

In relation to kyudo, one can say exactly the same thing. He who follows his master's instructions on the Way, who perseveres and practices seriously until he has assured himself of having the best technique and has arrived at its heights—this archer, through practicing his breathing over long years, will attain an ideal state in his concentration if he only continues increasing the tension of the body in the effort of the nobiai (tension + breathing + concentration). In this way it is possible to produce the form of the mind (the heart) in a natural way. If the archer tirelessly repeats this state, one day he will suddenly awaken, will discover that his own heart, just as it is, is the mind of the Bow. Nothing else will be contained in it, nothing else will be thought by it, it will be in the state of a newborn. He has mastered the details of the art; the complaints of his heart have become silent. Before the mato, his mind and body come together as one; in drawing the bow, the archer pours out of himself into the effort of shooting, and nonetheless, his technique is correct. This is the state that in Japan, from time immemorial, has been called *waza o suteru*, throwing away art, forgetting technique. Many faults and misunderstandings have arisen from regarding the meaning of these ancient words in only a superficial way.

This mind that is awakened by the Bow, that has opened the eyes and can now, with calm, cool judgment, see and observe shooting precisely, no longer fears mistakes. When mistakes try to sneak in anywhere, it appears on the spot immediately like a computer and fixes them. When, in the draw, the effort increases without interruption and under the mind's observation the perfection of the technique is intensified to the ultimate point, there comes the moment when the mind commands hanare. This mechanism of command, the physiological process and the energy that comes out of it, was not able to be demonstrated even by famous scientists, although most doctors concur in recognizing the existence of the phenomenon.

The mind of the archer works and exists in just the same way as the mind of a stone or a flower. His mind and the mind of the flower and the stone are not different. All work as one, in the same way.

The command for hanare, when will it come, when did it come? The mind (the heart) itself does not know. When it thinks about it after the shot, it doesn't find an answer.

To possess this mind, even without having a bow and arrow in one's hand, to participate in the life of this mind in everyday life, requires tireless practice. If the mind that is born through the Bow does not become one with everyday life, one has not reached actual enlightenment.

An ancient Chinese story recounts:

In ancient times the geese flew southward. But in China they gave a wide berth to the house of a famous master of archery, out of fear.

And now the other way around:

But when the master became quite old, a tiger actually made friends with him and became as tame as a dog. The geese had been afraid of him—that was in the time when he had discovered the Mind of the Bow, but it was not very developed yet. The tiger came to him—that was when this mind had penetrated into his daily life and had blended into him.

The mind that is born from practicing the Bow loves people, loves all things; it makes no distinction between things in and under heaven. It lives happily in this world, nothing frightens it; just as it is, its life comes to an end.

So may this mind, this heart, have its way.

GLOSSARY

Aibiki: Shooting at one another simultaneously.

ANKF: All-Nippon Kyudo Federation.

Aradame: Second stage in the rough straightening of the arrow shaft.

Ariake: "Rising moon"; image of how the target appears in relation to the bow.

Ashibumi: The stance, first stage of hassetsu.

Atari: A hit on the target.

Azuchi. Roofed target area with a raised sandbank to stop arrows.

Bondo: Glue.

Boshi: (1) Thumb-shaped cap worn in military shooting, (2) Thumb tip of the glove.

Botsunogi: A practice arrow without feathers.

Budo: General term for the Japanese martial arts.

Busha: Archery on foot.

Bushi: Japanese knight.

Bushi (fushi): Growth ring on bamboo.

Bushido: "Way of the Knight"; code of honor of the samurai.

Busuki: Shooting without enthusiasm and interest.

Chijimi: The right hand moving forward reducing the tension of the draw.

Chu: Penetrating force.

Daimyo: Title of high nobility.

Daisan: Second phase of the draw in the Ogasawara School, roughly corresponding to the sanbun no ni.

Dan: Literally, "stage"; one of ten degrees, starting with the 1st dan.

Deki bow: Bow with the bowstring to the left of its middle when viewed from above.

Do: "Way" in the sense of a lifelong practice; for example, kyudo, judo, kendo.

Doho: Two small pieces of wood used to make the nakashikake round.

Dojo: Practice hall.

Dokuya: Arrow with a poisoned tip.

Dosa: Movements before and after shooting.

Dozo: "Please," as in offering something.

Dozukuri: Balancing the torso, second stage of hassetsu.

Ebira: Open quiver worn on the hip.

Enteki: Distance shooting, at 60 m.

Fudeko: Powder for the bow hand.

Fujibanashi: Semicircular raw form of the bow.

Fukuzoyumi: The same as tsukuyumi—a bow with a hook to place the arrow on.

Fushikage: Shaft with shiny black lacquer on the bamboo rings and ring shadows.

Gi: kyudo shirt.

Ginteki: Silver target; see chap. 16, "Target Games."

Giriko: Glove powder.

Gomuyumi: Rubber practice "bow" for beginners.

Ha: (1) Branch school. (2) Feather placed on the arrow. (3) Distance between the bow and the string, 14–15 cm.

Hachiman: Shinto war god.

Hagi: Wrappings on an arrow.

Haiwo: Arrow tip in the shape of a fly's tail.

Hakama: Skirtlike trousers.

Hakama no kushita: Trapezoidal back piece of the hakama.

Hanare: Release, the eighth stage of hassetsu.

Hane: Feather.

Hankyu: Half bow.

Hanmato: "Half target" used for enteki shooting, 79 cm in diameter.

Hanshi: Highest honorary title for a teacher.

Haragawa: Leather piece on the thumb of a kyudo glove.

Hashimato: Star target.

Hassetsu: The eight basic stages of the shooting sequence.

Haya: First arrow in formal shooting.

Hayake: A premature release without the necessary physical and mental tension.

Hazu: Lower end of an arrow, the nock.

Heki Danjo Masatsugi: Founder of the Heki School, ca. 1440.

Heki Insai Ha: Branch of the Heki Ryu.

Heki Ryu: Heki school of kyudo.

Higo: Laminated piece, bow part.

Hijutsu: Secret art.

Hikae: Reinforced part of the glove that lies against the forearm.

Hikime: Ceremony in which a flute-headed arrow is shot.

Hikimenoya: Signal arrow, flute arrow.

Hikiwake: Drawing the bow with equal force left and right.

Himezori: The princess (upper) curve of the bow.

Hineri: A slight inward rotation of the right hand and forearm during kai.

Hinerigawa: Leather part of the glove.

Hinerikoto: Refers to the fast inward rotation of the right hand at the release.

Hirane: Literally, "flat arrowhead." A broad, turnip-shaped arrowhead.

Hitokoshi no saya: Set of 25, 20, or 16 war arrows.

Hitotsumato: Ceremonial shooting by three archers at one target.

Hiya: Flaming arrow.

Hokoya: Spear-shaped arrowhead.

Honda Ryu: Honda school of kyudo.

Honza: Base line for shooting in the dojo.

Hosha: Archery on foot.

Hoshikirifu: Star-spotted feather.

Hoshimato: Star target, 36 centimeters in diameter.

Hozuke: Contact of the arrow with the cheek in tsumeai.

Hsia: First Chinese dynasty, 1800 B.C.E.

Ichimonji: (1) Literally, the character 1, a groove in the glove placed at a right angle to the longitudinal axis of the thumb. (2) An arrow shaft that has the same diameter along its whole length.

Inuoi: Dog hunt.

Iriki bow: Bow with the bowstring to the right of its middle when viewed from above.

Ishiuchi: Literally, "stone striker"; tail feathers of the eagle.

Ite: Ancient term for an archer.

Itofu: Feather with threadlike markings.

Itohagi: Wrapping of thread at the end of the arrow.

Iwarimato: Rhombus 30 cm on a side used as a target in target games.

Jarai: Ceremonial shooting at the ancient imperial court.

Jindo: A type of hunting arrow.

Jun mokuroku: Quasi "Table of Contents"; first and lowest Heki school title.

Jutsu: Technique; art.

Kabahagi: Bark wrapping at the end of an arrow.

Kaburaya: Arrow with a bulge (kabura) on the shaft.

Kabuto: Large samurai helmet.

Kachiyumi: Archery on foot.

Kai: Full draw of the bow.

Kamihagi: Arrow wrapping of paper.

Kamiza: Divine seat; place of honor in the dojo, generally opposite the entrance.

Kan: Speed.

Kan chu kyu: Speed; penetrating force; endurance, continuity: motto of the Heki Ryu.

Kanteki: Caller at the target, who shouts the results of shooting to the kiroku.

Karabiki: "Empty drawing" of the bow before a training session.

Karahazu: The arrow falls to the ground at the release.

Karimata: Hunting arrow with a forked iron tip.

Kasumimato: "Mist target," 36 cm in diameter.

Katte: "Victory hand"; term for the right hand in the Ogasawara and Honda schools.

Kazuya: Historical method of rapid shooting.

Kendo: Way of the Sword; today also a sport.

Kenjutsu: Art of the sword.

Kiai: Battle cry.

Kinteki: Gold target.

Kiritsume: Point of contact on the bow between the bamboo and the inset wooden tip.

Kiroku: Recording clerk in competitions and examinations.

Kisha: Archery on horseback.

Kiza: Position of sitting on the heels with the left or right knee slightly raised.

Kohaku: Target game with a red and white target.

Kohimo: Thin leather strap on the glove.

Konari: Small curve of the bow.

Koshi: "Hip"; the thumb-side part of the glove.

Koshinari: The same as shimo no nari: the lower main curve of the bow.

Koshiya: "Hip arrow"; aimed shooting at a nearby enemy using an ebira.

Kozori: Small curve of the bow.

Kururiya: Hunting arrow with hollowed-out kabura (bulge).

Kyoshi: Second honorary title for a teacher.

Kyu: (1) "Class"; student degree running from the 5th to 1st kyu. (2) "Bow" in the Chinese pronunciation. (3) Endurance; continuity.

Kyudo: Way of the Bow.

Kyudojo: Kyudo practice hall.

Kyudoka: Kyudo practitioner, literally "expert"; better is *kyujin* ("bow person").

Kyuho: Handling of the bow.

Kyuki: Equipment lore.

Kyuko: Fabrication of the bow.

Kyurei: Ceremonies and forms of archery.

Kyuri: Theory of archery.

Magasune: String-rubbing device for warming up natural strings treated with resin.

Maha: "Genuine feather"; term for eagle feathers.

Makiwara: "Straw roll" for stopping arrows at a distance of 2–3 m.

Mamakiyumi: A composite, and later, a glued bow.

Marukiyumi: Bow made of whole sticks.

Marune: Massive round arrowhead.

Mato: Target, 36 cm in diameter.

Matoasobi: Target games.

Mato naoshimasu: "I adjust the mato."

Matotsuki: Literally, "pushing the target"; see chap. 14, "Competition Forms."

Matowaku: Wooden frame on which the omato is stretched.

Matoya: Arrow for mato shooting.

Meigen: "Sounding string"; luck-bringing ceremony.

Menpo: Frightening face mask of a samurai.

Mette: "Horse hand"; Heki Ryu term for the right hand in kyudo.

Mizunagare: Placing of the arrow in uchiokoshi and sanbun no ni.

Mochimato: Ceremonial shooting in which each archer shoots at his own target.

Mokuroku: "Table of Contents"; second title of the Heki school.

Mokuso: Concentration.

Momijigasane: Ideal form of the hand gripping the bow; literally, "maple leaf " or "baby's hand."

Mon; monsho: Family crest.

Monomi: "Looking at the target."

Monpuku: Under-kimono.

Morikawa Kosan: Master of the bow who first coined the expression "kyudo."

Motohazu: Lower tip of the bow.

Motokaburato: Wrapping of rattan (to) on the lower tip of the bow.

Motosekita: Inset wooden piece on the lower tip of the bow.

Motoshigeto: An early form of the to-wrapped bow.

Mugitsubo: "Grain of wheat"; arrow shaft that tapers at both ends.

Mugonka: "Song without Words"; third title of the Heki Ryu.

Munazuru: Contact between the string and the chest.

Muneate: Chest guard.

Naginata: Sword spear.

Nakadame: Straightening an arrow over fire.

Nakasashi: The lower arrow in traditional quivers.

Nakashikake: Nocking-point reinforcement.

Nami: The standard length of a bow.

Namihoko: Bow of standard length with a maximum draw of 82–83 cm.

Nari: The curved shape of the bow; also a general term for "shape."

Ne: Point.

Nejiru: Screwlike rotation, effort of the left hand.

Neru: First procedure in the rough forming of the arrow shaft.

Netsuke: Knob handle.

Nigiri: Bow grip.

Nigirigawa: Grip leather.

Ninja: Term for a spy during the feudal period.

No: Shaft.

Nobi: Bow with a maximum draw of 95 cm.

Nobiai: "Stretching"; seventh stage of hassetsu.

Nogoinono: Arrow with red lacquered shaft.

Nomine: Chisel-shaped arrowhead.

Noya: Hunting arrow.

Nurigometo no yumi: Term for the most common type of war bow.

Nuritsuru: Black lacquered string of a war bow.

Nuriyumi: Lacquered bow with any number of to wrappings.

O: "Large" strap on a kyudo glove.

Obi: Belt.

Ochi: Team leader.

Ogasawara Ryu: Ogasawara school of kyudo.

Oginomato: Fan target; see chap. 16, "Target Games."

Omato: "Large mato" for enteki: 158-cm diameter for ceremonies; 100-cm diameter for competitions.

Onegai shimasu: Literally, "please."

Onmato hajime: Ceremonial shooting for the New Year.

Osujikai: A form of glove with the string groove at an angle of 135 degrees to the longitudinal axis of the thumb.

Otoya: Second arrow in formal shooting.

Rei: Form, ceremony; also a command in the greeting ceremony.

Renshi: First honorary title for a teacher.

Renshin: Mind training.

Rokka: Six subjects of kyudo.

Ryu: School.

Saguri: Knotlike wrapping of the string above the nocking point.

Samurai: Warrior; warrior caste.

Sanbun no ni: "Second step of three"; fifth stage of hassetsu.

Sanjusangendo: Famous temple in Kyoto; literally, "thirty-three niches."

Sanzunzumari: Shortest bow (212 cm long), with a draw of less than 82 cm.

Sashiya: Piercing arrow.

Sawashino: Black lacquered shaft.

Seiza: Kneeling position.

Semenosekitsuru: Especially durable string with an extra wrapping of silk thread.

Senbontsuru: "Thousand-shot string" of plastic fiber (Kevlar).

Senjonoya: Battle arrow.

Sensei: Form of address for a teacher.

Seppuku: Ritual suicide performed by cutting open the belly.

Shai: Shooting or central line in a dojo.

Shaku: A measure of about 33 cm.

Sharei: Ceremonial shooting.

Shichigosan: "7-5-3"; see chap. 16, "Target Games."

Shigeto: Basic type of the first composite bows.

Shiko: Open quiver that can be hung on a belt by a hook.

Shime: Tranquilizer arrow for deer.

Shimohazu: Lower tip.

Shimononari: Lower curve of the bow.

Shin: Read as *mi* = body; read as *kokoro* = heart.

Shinanhyakushu: Fifth and highest title of the Heki Ryu: "One Hundred Songs of Instruction."

Shinto: Original religion of Japan, with elements of nature worship, ancestor cult, and patriotism.

Shinto no maki: "Way of the Gods" Scroll; fourth title of the Heki Ryu.

Shirano: Arrow with a shaft of natural color.

Shogun: Military commander of Japan.

Shoshin ni kaere: "Back to the enthusiasm of the beginner."

Shugyo taido: Attitude toward practice.

Shuraya: Arrow for fighting.

Sobaki: Wooden sides of a bow.

Soku: Unit of measure.

Soya: War arrow.

Suginari: "Cedar-shaped"; arrow with the greatest diameter at the tip.

Sujikai: Form of the string groove in the glove at an angle of 110 degrees to the lengthwise axis of the thumb.

Suyaki: Singed, brownish arrow.

Tabi: Socks.

Tachi: Long sword.

Tachirei: Standing bow.

Taihai: Set of movements (for example, at an examination).

Taikai: Competition.

Takeda Ryu: Takeda school of kyudo, which includes yabusame.

Takeyajiri: Arrow with bamboo tip.

Tanjohikime: Flute arrow shot for the birth of a child.

Tasuki: White cord for tying up the sleeve of a woman's kimono for sharei.

Tateichi: "Standing one"; see chap. 16, "Target Games."

Tekiwari: Perceiving the target, a competition form.

Temonkin: Line on the hand along which the left outer edge of the bow is placed.

Tenouchi: Form of the grip of the bow hand.

Tenranjiai: Competitive shooting in front of the emperor.

To: Rattan of the genus *calamus*, a composite-leafed palm; material used for wrappings on the bow.

Tobera: Spatula for glue work.

Togariya: War arrow with spear-shaped head.

Torafu: Feather with stripe markings.

Torikake: Taking hold of the string.

Toriuchi: Main curve of the bow ("bird striker").

Toshiya: Shooting competition of the Edo period.

Totokinoya: An arrow with poison on the feathered part of the shaft.

Tsugihazu: Shooting ring attached to the end of an arrow.

Tsumaguro: Black-edged feather.

Tsumeai: Sixth stage of hassetsu.

Tsunogi: Practice arrow.

Tsunomi: Part of the bow hand applied to the bow; literally, "looking at the horn."

Tsunomi no hataraki: The "work of the tsunomi."

Tsuru: Bowstring.

Tsurubukuro: Horseman's pouch for keeping bowstrings.

Tsurumaki: String roll, ring for holding spare strings.

Tsurumakura: "String cushion" on the kyudo glove.

Tsurune: Sound of the string at the release of the shot.

Tsurushirabe: Checking the string, an examination form.

Uaoshi: Pressing from above.

Uchiokoshi: Raising the bow; fourth hassetsu.

Urahazu: Upper tip of the bow.

Urakaburato: Rattan wrapping on the upper tip of the bow.

Urasekiita: Inset wooden piece on the upper tip of the bow.

Urushihagi: Lacquer-covered wrapping on an arrow.

Utsubo: Closed type of quiver.

Uwasashi: Upper arrow in the historical quiver.

Wakishomen: The same as kamiza; the front side.

Watakuri: "Gut ripper"; type of arrow with a barbed tip.

Watakushi: "Flesh cutter"; war arrow.

Ya: Arrow.

Ya agemasu: "I am retrieving the arrow."

Yabusame: Archery on horseback.

Yagoro: Part of eighth stage of hassetsu; continuation of the nobiai.

Yagoshihikime: Flute-arrow ceremony for healing a sick person.

Yami: "Full moon"; image of how the target appears when viewed by the archer in relation to the bow.

Yanagui: "Arrow biter"; framework on the ebira for holding arrows.

Yanochiku: Worked bamboo arrow shaft.

Yatate: Wooden container for storing arrows in the dojo.

Yazuka: Draw depth of the bow, corresponding normally to half the height of the archer's body.

Yazurito: Rattan wrapping on the bow grip.

Yazutsu: Arrow tube, the present-day form of the quiver.

Yohazu: Arrow end in the shape of a swallow's tail.

Yokoichi: "One on its side"; see chap. 16, "Target Games."

Yonsunnobi: Bow with a draw of over 96 cm.

Yu: A slight bow (in the sense of bowing at the waist).

Yudaoshi: Bringing the bow back to the hip.

Yugaeri: Rotation of the bow after hanare.

Yugake: Kyudo glove.

Yugamae: Readying the bow; third stage of hassetsu.

Yugi: A quiver with its opening on the top.

Yumi: Archer's bow.

Yumibukoro: Wrapper for the bow.

Yumitori: Ancient term for archer.

Yunde: Bow hand, the left hand.

Yurumi: "Slackness"; right arm moves in direction of target.

Zannen: Literally, "Too bad!"; a miss that touches the target.

Zanshin: Reflection; the form of body and mind left behind after the release of the shot.

Zazen: Sitting meditation.

Zen: School of Buddhism introduced into Japan from China in the thirteenth century by Dogen and Eisai, which strongly influenced the Japanese way of life and the arts.

Zen Nihon Kyudo Renmei: Pan-Japanese Kyudo Association, known in English as the All-Nippon Kyudo Federation (ANKF).

RECOMMENDED READING

Acker, William R. B. *Kyudo: The Japanese Art of Archery*. Rutland, Vermont and Tokyo: Charles E. Tuttle, 1998.

DeProspero, Dan and Jackie. *Illuminated Spirit: Conversations with a Kyudo Master*. Tokyo, New York, and London: Kodansha International, 1997.

Heath, E. G. *Grey Goose Wing: A History of Archery*. New York: New York Graphic Society, 1968.

Herrigel, Eugen. *Zen in the Art of Archery* (1952). Translated by R. F. C. Hull, with an introduction by D. T. Suzuki. New York: Vintage Books, 1999.

Hurst, G. Cameron III. *Armed Martial Arts of Japan: Swordsmanship and Archery*. New Haven, Conn.: Yale University Press, 1998.

Kushner, Kenneth. *One Arrow, One Life: Zen, Archery, Enlightenment*. Rutland, Vermont and Tokyo: Charles E. Tuttle, 2000.

Onuma, Hideharu. *Kyudo: The Essence and Practice of Japanese Archery*. Tokyo, New York, and London: Kodansha International, 1993.

Ratti, Oscar, and Adele Westbrook. *Secrets of the Samurai: A Survey of the Martial Arts of Feudal Japan*. Rutland, Vermont and Tokyo: Charles E. Tuttle, 1973; reissued 1991.

Sollier, André and Zsolt Györbiró. *Japanese Archery: Zen in Action*. New York and Tokyo: Walker/Weatherhill 1970.

Stein, Hans J. *Kyudo: The Art of Zen Archery*. London: Harper Collins, 1988.

ILLUSTRATION CREDITS

Photos of Inagaki Sensei on pages 225–26: Siegfried Gragnato, Stuttgart.

Fig. 1.5. Ogasawara Ryu: Thomas Schliewen, Trittau.

Fig. 6.4 was photographed by the author from a wall screen in the Tokyo National Museum.

Figs. 17.1 and 17.2. Military shooting: Angela Neumeister, Hamburg.

Fig. 17.3. Koshiyakiyumi: Fritz Nadler, Hamburg.

Fig. 17.4. Meigen ceremony: Waseda-Dojo, Tokyo.

All other photos and drawings were made by the author. Artworks (woodcuts, etc.) are from the author's collection.

RESOURCES

Information about kyudo is available from the following organizations:

American Kyudo Renme:
Dan DeProspero, President
501 Sleepy Valley Road
Apex, NC 27502
USA
email: *Kyudo@icomnet.com*

Dachverband der Heki-Kyudo-Schule e.V.
(Umbrella Organization of the Heki School)
c/o F. Hoff
Volksdorfer Weg 50r
D 22393 Hamburg
Germany

Zenko International
Kanjuro Shibata XX, Founder
4220 19th Street
Boulder, CO 80304
USA
phone/fax 303-544-9415
web: *www.zenko.org*
email: *zenko@interfold.com*

Zen Nihon Kyudo Renmei
Kishi Memorial Hall
1-1-1 Jinnan, Shibuya-ku
Tokyo, Japan